THE WARSAW GHETTO UPRISING

Striking a Blow Against the Nazis

The Holocaust Through Primary Sources

Linda Jacobs Altman

Enslow Publishers, Inc.
40 Industrial Road
Box 398
Berkeley Heights, NJ 07922
USA

http://www.enslow.com

Library of Congress Cataloging-in-Publication Data

Altman, Linda Jacobs, 1943–

The Warsaw Ghetto Uprising : striking a blow against the Nazis / Linda Jacobs Altman.

p. cm. — (The Holocaust through primary sources)

Summary: "Examines the Warsaw ghetto uprising, including the roots of the resistance in the Warsaw ghetto, stories from the participants in the uprising, how the battle ended, and how the small group of fighters became heroes during the Holocaust"—Provided by publisher.

Includes bibliographical references and index.

ISBN 978-0-7660-3320-7

1. Warsaw (Poland)—History—Warsaw Ghetto Uprising, 1943—Juvenile literature. 2. Holocaust, Jewish (1939-1945)—Poland—Warsaw—Juvenile literature. 3. Jews—Poland—Warsaw—History—20th century—Juvenile literature. I. Title.

D765.2.W3A76 2011

940.53'1853841—dc22

2010021596

Paperback ISBN 978-1-59845-347-8

Printed in China

052011 Leo Paper Group, Heshan City, Guangdong, China

10 9 8 7 6 5 4 3 2 1

To Our Readers: We have done our best to make sure all Internet Addresses in this book were active and appropriate when we went to press. However, the author and the publisher have no control over and assume no liability for the material available on those Internet sites or on other Web sites they may link to. Any comments or suggestions can be sent by e-mail to comments@enslow.com or to the address on the back cover.

Every effort has been made to locate all copyright holders of material used in this book. If any errors or omissions have occurred, please contact us at www.enslow.com. We will try to make corrections in future editions.

Permissions: Simha Rotem (Kazik), *Memoirs of a Warsaw Ghetto Fighter* (New Haven, Conn.: Yale University Press, 1994.) Reprinted with permission from Yale University Press, ©1994.

Illustration Credits: Associated Press, pp. 90, 102, 115; Enslow Publishers, Inc., p. 8; The Ghetto Fighters' House Photo Archive, pp. 36, 48, 62, 75; National Archives and Records Administration, p. 4; USHMM, pp. 7, 19, 27, 57, 64, 68, 73; USHMM, courtesy of Benjamin Meed, pp. 85, 88–89, 91, 93; USHMM, courtesy of Bildarchiv Preussischer Kulturbesitz, p. 45; USHMM, courtesy of Helmut Eschwege, p. 43; USHMM, courtesy of Leah Hammerstein Silverstein, pp. 25, 65; USHMM, courtesy of Leopold Page Photographic Collection, pp. 32, 96, 97; USHMM, courtesy of Louis Gonda, p. 109; USHMM, courtesy of National Archives and Records Administration, pp. 10, 17, 51, 76, 99, 106, 111, 113; USHMM, courtesy of Sophia Kalski, p. 70; USHMM, courtesy of Stadtarchiv Neustadt an der Weinstrasse, p. 6; USHMM, courtesy of YIVO Institute for Jewish Research, New York, p. 31; USHMM, courtesy of Zydowski Instytut Historyczny imienia Emanuela Ringelbluma, pp. 80, 83; USHMM, courtesy of Zydowski Instytut Historyczny Instytut Naukowo-Badawczy, pp. 40, 54; Yad Vashem Photo Archives, p. 21; Yad Vashem Photo Archives / Stadtarchiv Muenchen, p. 12.

Cover Illustration: Public Domain Image (Nazi soldiers force Jews captured during the Warsaw ghetto uprising to the assembly point for deportation in May 1943); USHMM, courtesy of Fritz Gluckstein (Star of David artifact).

Contents

INTRODUCTION

I n the city of Warsaw, Poland, in April 1943, about two hundred Jewish partisans prepared for a battle they could never hope to win. These fighters, mostly young and untrained, were beyond caring about winning or losing. The German occupational forces had imprisoned them in a disease-ridden ghetto, behind an eleven-foot wall made of brick and barbed wire. Thousands of Jews had already starved to death or fallen victim to epidemic disease. Tens of thousands had been sent away in boxcars, never to be seen again.

German soldiers force a group of Jews captured during the Warsaw ghetto uprising to march to the assembly point for deportation in May 1943. The fighting between the German soldiers and the Jewish resistance lasted for twenty-eight days.

The Germans had combat-trained soldiers and a huge arsenal of weapons. The partisans had only the expectation of death, the determination to go down fighting, and a certain element of surprise; the last thing the Germans would expect was a fight from a ragtag band of untrained rebels.

The first Germans through the gate of the ghetto walked into a firestorm of bullets and bombs. Jewish insurgents shot from the windows of surrounding buildings. They raced over the rooftops, flinging grenades and firebombs into the chaotic street below. The Germans fell back in confusion. Against all odds, the battle they never expected was both real and deadly.

The fighting would last for twenty-eight days, and, in that time, would touch every life in the ghetto: resistance fighters and their allies, Jews who had feared provoking the Nazis, the starving masses who were too far gone to care. It touched the Nazis as well, giving them a hard lesson about fighting an enemy with nothing left to lose. The experiences of all these people not only tell the story of the uprising, but also put a human face on one of the most inhuman periods in history.

The roots of the Warsaw ghetto uprising can be traced back to the German invasion of Poland on September 1, 1939, when World War II began. Just twenty-seven days later, the victorious German army marched into the city of Warsaw and established a military government. The occupation would be harsh, especially for a Jewish community that numbered more than 350,000.

German dictator Adolf Hitler regarded Jews as evil and dangerous. He claimed that they threatened the superior "Aryan" race, as he called the German people. He blamed Jews and other "subhuman" groups for Germany's woes, from the loss of World War I to the punitive treaty imposed by the victors, and the crumbling economy that plagued Germany during the Great Depression of the 1930s. To combat this "threat," the Nazis forced Jews to the fringes of society and later tried to destroy them altogether.

By the time Nazi forces invaded Poland, German Jews had already suffered terribly under Hitler's rule. They had lost their jobs, their homes, and their businesses. In November 1935, they lost their German citizenship. Polish Jews could expect more of the same. Less than a week after the fall of Warsaw, the

A troupe of carnival actors march in an antisemitic parade mocking Jewish life in Germany. The float in the parade shows a burning synagogue. Jews in Germany suffered terribly under the rule of Adolf Hitler, and Polish Jews suffered the same fate after Germany's invasion on September 1, 1939.

Jews in Warsaw were forced to wear a white armband with a blue Star of David to identify themselves.

German military government established a *Judenrat,* or Jewish council, to carry out their orders in the Jewish community. A long list of repressive measures soon followed. Jews had to identify themselves with armbands bearing the six-pointed Star of David. They had to identify their businesses with "Jewish owned" signs in the windows. More regulations followed: Jews could not hold government jobs, employ Gentiles (non-Jews) in their homes and businesses, or even ride on trains without special permission. Jewish males between the ages of sixteen and sixty had to register for forced labor and work for the Nazis without payment.

The hardest blow came in October 1940: all Jews in Warsaw had to leave their homes and move into a shabby neighborhood of pockmarked streets and bleak tenements. From every part of the city, Jewish families came, laden with whatever belongings they could carry. They crowded into substandard apartments, often without sanitary facilities or heat.

GHETTOS IN
OCCUPIED EUROPE
1939–1944

0   250 Miles
0   250KM

1944 International Boundaries
German-Occupied
German Ally
Liberated/Allies
Neutral Countries
Date Ghettos Established
○ 1939–May 1941
◎ June 1941–1943
● 1944

The Nazis forced all of Warsaw's Jews to move into the ghetto in October 1940. During the Holocaust, the Nazis established at least one thousand ghettos for Jews, mostly in Eastern Europe. This map shows some of the major ghettos in German-occupied Europe.

In November, the Germans closed off the ghetto with a brick wall more than eleven feet high, topped with barbed wire and broken glass. Behind the wall, Jewish life entered a new and deadly phase. The Germans turned the ghetto into a death trap, with starvation rations and poor sanitation. They used it as a source of slave labor. Thousands of Jews died from overwork, starvation, and epidemic disease. By the summer of 1942, the Germans were packing Jews into boxcars like cordwood and transporting them to unknown destinations.

Confusion and despair gripped the people of the ghetto. Some held on to fading hopes of better times to come. Others gave up and merely suffered in silence. Still others decided to fight back. They did not expect to win, but they vowed to make the Nazis pay dearly for every Jewish life lost in that grim place behind the wall.

Adam Czerniakow: The Chairman

Adam Czerniakow was born in Warsaw on November 30, 1880. As the son of a prosperous family, he received a good education and became an industrial engineer. It was not a spectacular life, but it was a good one: satisfying work, a wife and child, and social standing in the Jewish community. Then came September 1, 1939, and the German invasion of Poland.

Poland reeled under a brutal attack—tanks and mortars from the ground, bombs from the sky. German leader Adolf Hitler

German soldiers march through Warsaw on October 5, 1939, celebrating their conquest of Poland. Life would change quickly for Jews in Warsaw living under Nazi occupation.

had a name for it: *blitzkrieg*, or "lightning war." Polish resistance crumbled, and on September 28, 1939, German troops marched into Warsaw.

As soon as the occupational authorities set up an office, Adam Czerniakow went to them and volunteered to become chairman of the Jewish community. He knew that occupational governments usually worked through existing agencies and officials. After many years of experience as a community leader, he considered himself equal to the task. Had he known what lay ahead, he might not have asked for the job.

Living Under Nazi Occupation

Czerniakow's first task was to create a Judenrat, a council of twenty-four Jews and an equal number of alternates, to deal with the day-to-day affairs of the Jewish community. He would answer to the *Schutzstaffel* (SS), an elite special security force known for its brutal methods. They made it clear that the Judenrat would exist for one purpose and one purpose only: to carry out German orders. Czerniakow accepted this because he had no other choice.

He hoped to sidestep disaster long enough for the Jewish community of Warsaw to survive the war. That would mean walking a narrow line between obedience to the Nazis and activism on behalf of the Jews.

More often than not, Czerniakow's efforts failed, but he kept hoping that "next time" would be better. He achieved just enough success to keep that hope alive in spite of the terrible misery he saw around him. One of his early successes involved labor gangs.

The Germans got workers by snatching Jews off the streets. Any Jewish male could end up doing hours of hard physical labor without pay and often without food.

Czerniakow knew he could not stop labor conscription and he did not even try. Instead, he limited himself to achieving what he thought was possible. He offered the SS a bargain; the Judenrat would supply five hundred workers a day in exchange for an end

Adam Czerniakow reads a document in the Judenrat office. Czerniakow did his best to claim small victories with the SS, such as ending random labor conscription.

to random conscription. The Germans agreed. Czerniakow's plan reduced the number of rude surprises on the street and allowed Jews to prepare for their workdays.

On November 4, 1939, an SS soldier walked into the Judenrat offices unannounced and ordered a council meeting for three o'clock that afternoon. All council members and alternates should be in attendance. When some people could not be reached, the SS ordered Czerniakow to complete the list by any means necessary: "We enlisted people who happened to be around," he wrote in his diary.[1]

The Germans talked about confining all Jews in what they called a "zone of settlement." Czerniakow called it a ghetto, and the thought of being isolated from the rest of society horrified him. At that particular meeting, the SS did not pursue the matter, but Czerniakow did not forget. The threat of a ghetto would nag at him in the days to come.

As the meeting drew to a close, its real purpose came to light. A detachment of SS soldiers appeared to take the twenty-four council alternates into custody. As hostages of war, these men would guarantee the "good behavior" of the Jewish community. Any resistance, any violence, would get them killed.

This policy of collective responsibility put all Jews at risk, not just the hostages. In the event of any attack on German soldiers, or German institutions, the SS would drag innocent Jews from their homes and execute them without trial.

Tragedy on Nalewki Street

The Nazis did not waste time putting the collective responsibility rule into effect. On November 13, 1939, Jewish women from an apartment house at 9 Nalewki Street descended upon Czerniakow's office in a panic. A Jewish suspect ran into their building, where he attacked two Polish policemen, wounding one and killing the other. Before the residents realized what was happening, SS troops raided 9 Nalewki Street and dragged all fifty-three male residents off to jail. The women begged Czerniakow to save their husbands, fathers, and brothers.

They did not seem to understand that a Jewish chairman had no real power under a Nazi government. Czerniakow understood it all too well. Still, he promised to see what he could do. He approached the SS, who promised to release the Nalewki prisoners for 300,000 zlotys (Polish currency). In 1939, that was more than 1.5 million American dollars.

Czerniakow delivered 100,000 zlotys on November 24, and 142,000 zlotys on the twenty-fifth. He was granted permission to deliver the remaining 38,000 zlotys on the following Monday.

When he arrived with the last payment, an official told him that the men from Nalewki Street had already been shot. Czerniakow had not expected such behavior, even from the Nazis. In his upper-middle-class world, people were polite, predictable, and always kept their word. The task of informing the families fell to Czerniakow. He wrote in his diary:

> *I summoned the waiting families into my office in the presence of one councilor (the others were only too happy to take advantage of my offer to leave). A scene very difficult to describe. The wretched people in confusion. Then bitter recriminations against me. I left the Community at 1:30. The poor creatures were clinging to the carriage. What could I have done for them?[2]*

The best Czerniakow could do for the Nalewki families was to bring the bodies of their dead relatives home. That was a very difficult task. For weeks, the Germans refused to tell him where they had buried the bodies. They would not disclose the site until April 1940.

Signs of Things to Come

Some five months after the Nalewki burials, the ghetto Czerniakow had tried to avoid became a reality. The SS ordered all Jews to move into a run-down neighborhood within the city. When Czerniakow realized that he could not avoid the ghetto, he did what he had always done: accepted the facts and focused on the possible. He developed a plan for this new neighborhood, asking permission for many improvements: a larger area, better boundaries, financing for social service programs, and permission to open schools.

In his effort to make the best of a bad situation, Czerniakow may have pushed too hard. On November 4, 1940, two SS men bashed into the community offices and started brutally beating several members of the staff. Czerniakow's diary tells what happened after that:

At 3:30 I heard battering at the front door and the sound of windows being broken. A soldier with an officer . . . entered the building and . . . proceeded to beat Popover, First, etc. . . . I called the Gestapo and was instructed to get one of the armed men to the telephone. I called on a soldier who happened to be nearby but he refused in an irritated tone, ordering me to follow him. When I appeared in the Battalion office, the officer in charge set upon me, hitting me on the head until I fell. At this point the soldiers started kicking me with their boots. When I tried to stand up they jumped on me and threw me down the stairs. Half a flight down they beat me again. . . . I was [later taken] to Pawiak [prison].[3]

The ghetto turned out to be far worse than Czerniakow had expected. The Nazis forced 300,000 Jews into an area about the size of New York City's Central Park.[4] That number swelled to 400,000 when Jews from surrounding villages and towns were relocated to Warsaw. An average of seven people lived in each run-down apartment, often without a private bathroom.

The Germans soon enclosed this misbegotten neighborhood behind eleven-foot-high brick walls topped with barbed wire and shards of broken glass. To add insult to injury, the Nazis forced the Jewish community to pay for and to help build the wall.

This is the Jewish Council building in ruins after the Warsaw ghetto uprising. On November 4, 1940, the SS stormed into this building and attacked several members of the Judenrat, including Adam Czerniakow.

Behind the Ghetto Walls

Czerniakow scrambled to bring order to this chaos. In a matter of weeks, he put together a bureaucracy to keep the ghetto running. He set up agencies for everything from food procurement to public sanitation. By order of the Germans, he also created a Jewish police force, staffing it from a pool of volunteers. As a group, the police tended to be young, out of touch with Jewish tradition, and hardened to the misery of life behind the walls.

In one of his most controversial acts, Czerniakow appointed Jozef Szerynski as police force commander. The people of the ghetto despised Szerynski because he had renounced Judaism and become a Christian. Czerniakow ignored their protests. He was not concerned about the man's religion, only about his professional experience. Szerynski had been an officer in the Polish police force; for Czerniakow, that was reason enough to choose him for the job.

As a secular (non-religious) Jew, he was surprised by the outrage in the community. Orthodox Jews, as well as many liberals, despised Szerynski, the convert, as a traitor to his people. To Czerniakow's dismay, Szerynski hated the people as much as they hated him.

Under his leadership, the ghetto police became corrupt and cruel. Many engaged in bribery, thievery, blackmail, and intimidation. Despite public opinion, Czerniakow defended his choice to the bitter end. That end came in May 1942, when the Germans arrested Szerynski for smuggling furs out of the ghetto.

The Nazis forced the Jews to pay for and to construct the walls around the Warsaw ghetto. In this photo, Jewish and Polish laborers build a section of the wall.

With a corrupt police force adding to the misery, ghetto life went from bad to worse. People lived in filth, died of typhus, which was spread by lice, and other maladies that came from polluted drinking water. Living skeletons wandered the streets, some so far gone that they no longer felt hungry. Every morning, a funeral cart made the rounds and returned with a load of corpses.

Enemies at the Crossroads

While the ghetto died around him, Czerniakow continued to struggle against overwhelming odds. He still believed that rebellion of any kind would only give the Nazis an excuse for slaughtering more Jews. It would be some time before he realized that the Nazis did not need an excuse.

By the spring of 1942, young people in the ghetto were beginning to realize what Czerniakow could not see—that the policy of cooperation with the Germans was doomed to failure. The answer, they believed, was active and passive resistance to German policies. They developed an underground press, calling for Jews to defy German directives whenever possible.

Czerniakow cautioned them that their activities could get hundreds, even thousands, of innocent people killed. Communal responsibility loomed large in Czerniakow's memory. He could not forget the men of Nalewki Street, or the many others who had died for the actions of a stranger.

Despite the mounting death toll, he still believed that cooperating with SS directives would save the community as a whole. The young people did not see it that way, so in spite of

Bekanntmachung

Betr.: Todesstrafe für unbefugtes Verlassen der jüdischen Wohnbezirke.

In der letzten Zeit ist durch Juden, die die ihnen zugewiesenen Wohnbezirke verlassen haben, in zahlreichen Fällen nachweislich das Fleckfieber verbreitet worden. Um die hierdurch der Bevölkerung drohende Gefahr abzuwenden, hat der Herr Generalgouverneur verordnet, dass in Zukunft ein Jude, der den ihm zugewiesenen Wohnbezirk unbefugt verlässt, mit dem Tode bestraft wird.

Die gleiche Strafe trifft diejenigen, die diesen Juden wissentlich Unterschlupf gewähren oder in anderer Weise (z. B. durch Gewährung von Nachtlagern, Verpflegung, Mitnahme auf Fahrzeugen aller Art usw.) den Juden behilflich sind.

Die Aburteilung erfolgt durch das Sondergericht Warschau.

Ich weise die gesamte Bevölkerung des Distrikts Warschau auf diese neue gesetzliche Regelung ausdrücklich hin, da nunmehr mit unerbittlicher Strenge vorgegangen wird.

Warschau, am 10. November 1941.

gez. Dr. FISCHER
Gouverneur

Obwieszczenie

Dotyczy: kary śmierci za nieuprawnione opuszczenie żydowskich dzielnic mieszkaniowych.

W ostatnim czasie rozprzestrzenili żydzi, którzy opuścili wyznaczone im dzielnice mieszkaniowe, w licznych udowodnionych wypadkach tyfus plamisty. Aby zapobiec grożącemu w ten sposób niebezpieczeństwu dla ludności, rozporządził Generalny Gubernator, że żyd, który w przyszłości opuści nieuprawniony wyznaczoną mu dzielnicę mieszkaniową, będzie karany śmiercią.

Tej samej karze podlega ten, kto takim żydom udziela świadomie schronienia lub im w inny sposób pomaga (np. przez udostępnienie noclegu, utrzymania, przez zabranie na pojazdy wszelkiego rodzaju itp.).

Osądzenie nastąpi przez Sąd Specjalny w Warszawie.

Zwracam całej ludności Okręgu Warszawskiego wyraźnie uwagę na to nowe postanowienie ustawowe, ponieważ odtąd będzie stosowana bezlitosna surowość.

Warszawa, dnia 10 listopada 1941.

(—) Dr FISCHER
Gubernator

The SS posted this notice in Warsaw imposing the death penalty for any Jew attempting to leave the ghetto. As the death toll began to mount, some younger residents in the ghetto began to believe that cooperating with SS laws was not going to save the Jewish community.

Czerniakow's warnings, they held secret meetings and churned out pamphlets and newsletters, calling upon the people of the ghetto to resist their oppressors in any way possible.

When the Germans learned that underground literature was circulating through the ghetto, they took immediate action. On April 17, 1942, the Nazis executed fifty-one Jews for pamphleteering and other underground activities.

Czerniakow did not find out about the executions until the next day. This was a one-time "*aktion*," the SS told him. Jews could go about their work without fear of another mass killing.

Less than three months later, on July 2, another "one-time aktion" took place. The Nazis executed one hundred Jewish civilians and ten ghetto policemen. The policemen were charged with bribery and other crimes. The civilians died because someone they never knew had attacked a German policeman. Once more, the SS assured Czerniakow that there would be no further executions.

Just twenty days later, on July 22, the SS announced that: "all the Jews irrespective of sex and age, with certain exceptions, will be deported to the East."[5] They ordered Czerniakow to provide six thousand people by four o'clock in the afternoon.

For the next day, the SS demanded nine thousand people, most of them children.

When the SS told Czerniakow to sign the deportation order, he asked for a few minutes to consider the matter. He calmly went into his office and swallowed poison. A few minutes later, a staff member found Czerniakow slumped over his desk, with a note at his side: "They are demanding that I kill the children of my people with my own hands. There is nothing for me to do but die."[6]

After Czerniakow's suicide, the Judenrat faltered. They realized that cooperation with the Germans would not work, but they still believed that any form of rebellion would doom the ghetto to destruction. At this time of grief and fear, the underground began moving into the void. New voices spoke out, telling the ghetto that it was time to fight.

ADAM CZERNIAKOW'S SUICIDE

From the beginning of his chairmanship, Adam Czerniakow provoked controversy. Some said he was indecisive and cowardly; others considered him an honest man, doing the best he could under intolerable circumstances. Ghetto diarist Chaim Kaplan took both positions.

On September 17, 1940, he labeled Czerniakow "a mediocre man" who served the SS rather than the Jewish people. Three days after Czerniakow's suicide, Kaplan changed his view:

The first victim of the deportation decree was . . . Adam Czerniakow, who committed suicide by poison in the Judenrat building. . . . [A]fter his death, the reason became clear. [He] had refused to sign the expulsion order. He followed the Talmudic law: if someone comes to kill me, using might and power, and turns a deaf ear to all my pleas, he can do to me whatever his heart desires, since he has the power, and strength always prevails. But to give my consent, to sign my own death warrant— this no power on earth can force me to do, not even the brutal force of the foul-souled Nazi. . . . [Czerniakow] did not have a good life, but he had a beautiful death. . . . There are those who earn immortality in a single hour. . . . Adam Czerniakow earned his immortality in a single instant.[7]

2 Mordechai Anielewicz: The Commander

Mordechai Anielewicz was born in 1919 in the town of Wyszkow, near Warsaw. As the son of a working-class Jewish family, Mordechai faced two problems growing up: poverty and the widespread antisemitism that forced Polish Jews to the fringes of society. Even before the Nazis came to Poland, Jews suffered from harsh antisemitism. Stung by the near-constant discrimination, Mordechai became part of the Zionist youth movement, working to reestablish a Jewish homeland in Palestine.

After graduating from high school, he quickly joined a Zionist youth group called *Hashomer Hatzair* (Hebrew for "Youth Guard") and became a tireless organizer for the cause. He expected the Jewish homeland to become his lifework—until World War II got in the way.

When Germany conquered Poland in September 1939, an elite special security force known as the SS occupied Warsaw. Under this strict military government, Jews were more or less free to move about the city, or even to travel outside it. Mordechai Anielewicz used this time to step up his organizing efforts for Zionism. He worked with a new sense of urgency, trying to make the Zionist movement strong enough to last through the German occupation.

Mordechai Anielewicz (back row, right) stands for a portrait with other members of Hashomer Hatzair in Warsaw in 1938. Anielewicz joined the Zionist youth group after graduating from high school.

In the Ghetto

Anielewicz lost his freedom of movement when the "Jewish quarter," as the SS called the ghetto, was established and sealed. Inside the walls, Jewish life entered a new and deadly phase, with starvation and epidemic disease as daily realities.

The Judenrat could do nothing. Here and there, chairman Adam Czerniakow won small concessions, but the death rate kept rising. In spite of this, the Judenrat insisted that compliance with German orders offered the best chance of survival. With no evidence to the contrary, the people of the ghetto went along with that idea. Then Germany invaded the Soviet Union and reports of killing squads that slaughtered whole Jewish communities filtered back to Warsaw.

Anielewicz hoped that this news would be a wake-up call for the Judenrat. When they discounted it, he began a sustained effort to transform Hashomer Hatzair into a resistance movement. He became more aggressive in his organizing efforts, reaching out to potential allies and building an arsenal of weapons for the time when the Jews of Warsaw would have to fight.

The Beginning

Anielewicz did not confine his recruiting efforts to Warsaw. He went to other Jewish communities seeking young people willing to stand against the Germans. While he was away on this recruiting mission, tragedy gripped the ghetto. Between July 22 and September 12, 1942, the Nazis sent 265,000 Jews to their deaths

In the Warsaw ghetto, Mordechai Anielewicz began transforming Hashomer Hatzair into a resistance movement. He traveled throughout Warsaw and the surrounding communities searching for members. This is a map of the Warsaw ghetto showing some of the important places.

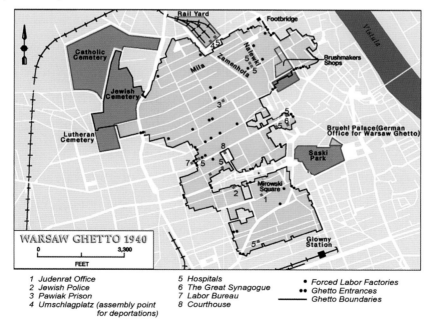

WARSAW GHETTO 1940

0   3,300

FEET

1 Judenrat Office
2 Jewish Police
3 Pawiak Prison
4 Umschlagplatz (assembly point for deportations)

5 Hospitals
6 The Great Synagogue
7 Labor Bureau
8 Courthouse

• Forced Labor Factories
•• Ghetto Entrances
—— Ghetto Boundaries

in the gas chambers of Treblinka. Another 11,580 went to work camps, and about 10,000 died, or were killed, in the ghetto. In the midst of this horror, representatives of several youth groups met to form the Jewish Combat Organization, *Zydowska Organizacja Bojowa* (ZOB).[1] It was little more than a name when Anielewicz returned to the ghetto. He joined and soon made the ZOB his personal mission in life.

The Enemy Within

In the aftermath of the "great deportation," as it came to be called, the ZOB decided to take action. They began by dealing with traitors within the ghetto: collaborators, informers, and most of all, the Jewish police. Without the ghetto police force, the Nazis could not have deported three hundred thousand people in less than two months. Not only did the police round up people and load them into boxcars, they did so with the utmost brutality.

Outraged at the ghetto police and other collaborators, many in the ZOB wanted to start random executions of Jewish policemen. Anielewicz refused to employ the same principle of collective guilt that the Germans had used to such deadly effect. Not only would this be immoral, he claimed, it would be a waste of scarce resources. Executing high-profile leaders for cause and in public would have a greater effect than random killings.

Soon after these discussions, the ZOB pronounced death sentences on several key people, including ghetto police chief Josef Szerynski and his second-in-command, Yakov Lejkin. The group sent to execute Szerynski only succeeded in wounding him.

Even though the attack served notice that things were changing in the ghetto, the ZOB considered it a failure. They vowed to do better with Szerynski's deputy.

The task of planning the Lejkin execution fell to Mordechai Anielewicz. In keeping with the principles he had helped to set, he wanted to execute Lejkin publicly and let the whole ghetto know why. He assigned ZOB operatives to shadow Lejkin and learn his habits. When they had compiled enough information, they chose their place and time for the execution—busy Gesia Street—before sundown. On October 29, Eliahu Rozanski, who had been one of Lejkin's "shadows," carried out the execution and made a clean getaway.

Anielewicz and his comrades immediately issued a statement:

> We would like to inform the public that as a consequence of the sentence imposed on the . . . officers, and personnel of the [Jewish police] . . . the judgment against [Yakov Lejkin], deputy commander . . . was executed on the 29th of October, at 6 p.m.[2]

Mordechai Anielewicz as a Leader

With the Lejkin execution, Anielewicz demonstrated his ability for careful planning combined with bold action. He proved equally adept at recruiting other Jewish youth groups into the cause. He succeeded where others had failed, because he did not even try to smooth over every ideological difference. He used another tack, reminding the young fighters that all of them shared a common enemy. They also shared a conviction that sooner or later, they would have to fight that enemy in a life-or-death confrontation.

Though Anielewicz's leadership abilities played an important part in the growth of ZOB, so did the changing mood in the ghetto. Adam Czerniakow was dead, and many other older leaders perished during the great deportation. With only 35,000 Jews left in the ghetto, the voice of defiant youth spoke out, and people were listening.

Anielewicz became commander of the ZOB in November 1942. He no longer had to worry about recruiting—new members filled out the ranks. He did have to worry about getting enough weapons for them. In German-occupied Poland, both Poles and Jews could be shot for owning a gun. When the underground tried to buy weapons, every firearm in Warsaw seemed to disappear. Some Polish freedom fighters supplied a few, but Anielewicz learned that he could not depend on them as a source. Many Polish groups did not have enough weapons for their own people. Others simply refused to deal with Jews.

The January Uprising

Without decent weapons, the ZOB command staff could not plan a sustained attack against the enemy. Anielewicz hoped for enough time to arm and train the Jewish fighters. But time turned out to be a luxury that he did not have. On January 18, 1943, the Germans began another round of deportations. Anielewicz and his

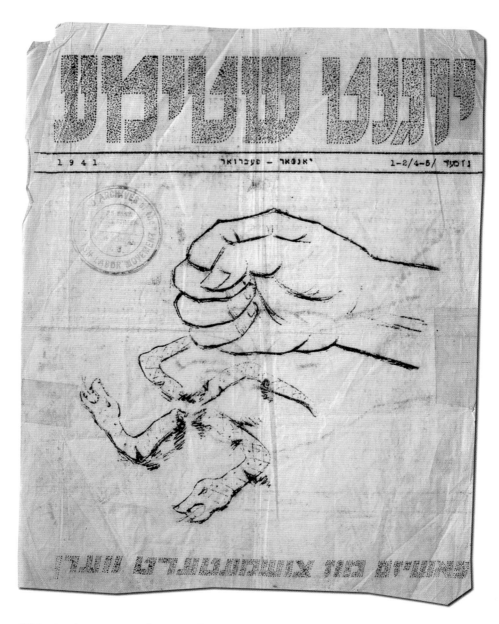

This is the cover of an underground Yiddish newspaper called *Voice of Youth* circulated in the Warsaw ghetto between January and February 1941. The headline at the bottom reads: "Fascism must be smashed." The ZOB used the underground newspaper and other pamphlets to get out their message of resistance.

people refused to stand by and do nothing while thousands more went to the gas chambers of Treblinka.

With little time for reflection, Anielewicz planned a limited action that would rely upon stealth and surprise more than weaponry. When Jews gathered in the *Umschlagplatz*, the place of assembly for deportations, twelve fighters with pistols slipped into the deportation lines, spacing themselves far enough apart

A German soldier leads a group of Jews to the railway depot during the great deportation. During the January uprising, the ZOB had fighters infiltrate the deportation lines and start a battle with the Germans.

for maximum effect. At a given signal, each fighter attacked the nearest soldier. In the confusion, many of the Jews in the deportation lines managed to escape. Most of the twelve ZOB fighters died that day.

Anielewicz managed to overpower a soldier and take his rifle. Then he hid in a bombed-out building, not knowing where else to go. Before he quite knew what was happening, somebody grabbed him and pulled him into a bunker, or underground shelter. He found himself among friends: a group of Jews in hiding, who seemed fascinated to see one of their own carrying a weapon.

The January insurrection became a turning point for Anielewicz and the ZOB. Their bold action inspired the people of the ghetto and served notice that Jews would no longer be passive victims. For the first time, Germans entered the ghetto cautiously, watching for signs of partisan activity.

The Ghetto Fights

After the January uprising, a new sense of purpose animated the ghetto, as people looked to the underground they had once despised. Anielewicz did not give them comforting messages about the days to come. In an open letter to the ghetto, he simply told them the truth:

> On January 22, 1943, six months will have passed since the deportations from Warsaw began. We all remember well the days of terror during which 300,000 of our brothers

and sisters were cruelly put to death in the death camp of Treblinka. . . . Today we must understand that the Nazi murderers have let us live only because they want to make use of our capacity to work. . . . We are slaves. And when the slaves are no longer profitable, they are killed. Every one among us must understand that, and every one among us must remember it always. . . .

Jews in your masses, the hour is near. You must be prepared to resist, not to give yourselves up like sheep to slaughter. Not even one Jew must go to the train. People who cannot resist actively must offer passive resistance, that is, by hiding. . . . Now our slogan must be: Let everyone be ready to die like a man!³

At dawn on April 19, two thousand enemy troops marched into the ghetto in tight, military formation. They planned to "liquidate," or destroy, the ghetto in short order, as a birthday present for Adolf Hitler. The street was empty and silent until a lone Jewish girl stepped out of a doorway and lobbed a grenade into their midst. The Germans scattered in disarray. They were regular army, trained for battlefield conditions. Nothing had prepared them for the unpredictable tactics of guerilla warfare.

Anielewicz had the partisans shooting from the windows of burned-out buildings. The resistance fighters raced over the rooftops throwing grenades and lightbulb bombs. They appeared suddenly from doorways or alleys to shoot down enemy soldiers and take their weapons.

That day, the ZOB forced a whole German detachment out of the ghetto. As the fighting went into a second day, then a third, and beyond, scarcity of weapons was not the only organizational problem Anielewicz faced. With no reliable means of communication, each fighting group had to operate alone. They could not coordinate their separate activities and this made it difficult to plan attacks.

On the fifth day of fighting, Anielewicz happened upon a smugglers' den, a large and well-appointed bunker at Mila 18. Under the direction of one Shmuel Asher, the residents of this place made a living by dealing in contraband goods. Like most people engaging in illegal activities, Asher was suspicious of strangers. When he found out that his uninvited guest was commander of the ZOB, the suspicions disappeared. Asher offered to share his bunker with the ZOB command staff. Anielewicz gladly accepted.

Having a somewhat permanent headquarters made operations a little easier. However, it did not stop the steady march of time. Each day, the struggle grew more and more difficult; each day, the Germans pounded the ghetto harder than before. Each day, Anielewicz and his brave comrades realized that their time was running out.

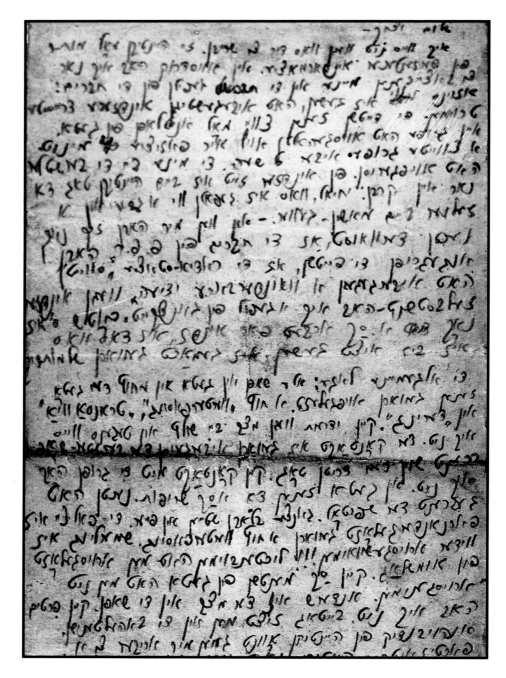

A copy of the last letter written by Mordechai Anielewicz given to Yitzhak Zuckerman.

Last Words

By May, the Germans were burning the ghetto building by
building and street by street, forcing hidden Jews into the open.
They found Mila 18 on May 8. As they broke through, Anielewicz
shot himself and his girlfriend, Mira Fuchrer. He left no written
statement behind. As far as anyone knows, the closest Anielewicz
came to summing up his life and impending death was his letter to
Yitzhak Zuckerman, dated April 23, 1943:

It is impossible to put into words what
we have been through. One thing is clear,
what happened exceeded our boldest
dreams. The Germans ran twice from the
ghetto. One of our companies held out
for 40 minutes and another for more
than 6 hours. The mine we set in the
[manufacturing district] exploded. Several
of our companies attacked the dispersing
Germans. . . . The dream of my life has
risen to become fact. Self defense in the
ghetto will have been a reality. Jewish
armed resistance and revenge are facts.
I have been a witness to the magnificent,
heroic fighting of Jewish men in battle.[4]

3 Yitzhak Zuckerman: An Ongoing Struggle

Yitzhak Zuckerman was born in December 1915, in Vilna, Lithuania. As the son of Zionists and grandson of a rabbi, he attended a grammar school run by the religious Zionist movement and a secular high school with a reputation for academic excellence. After high school, Yitzhak was accepted by two excellent colleges, but he chose a different path—joining the Jewish youth movement and training for emigration to Palestine.

"This Is How I Left"

Zuckerman soon became an organizer for *He-Halutz* (Hebrew for "the pioneer"). After the Nazi invasion of Poland in 1939, He-Halutz began positioning its organizers to keep the Zionist movement alive. They assigned Zuckerman to the city of Kowel, in the Soviet zone. He had to leave Vilna so quickly that he could only manage a brief visit with his parents:

That hasty departure from Vilna to Kowel haunted me for a long time. I didn't know it would be the last time I would see my parents and our home. Father said he didn't understand the point of my trip. . . .

He would have understood if I had gone closer to Eretz Israel. But to go farther away? I couldn't tell him that I was going to do clandestine work. . . . I shall never forget the picture: Mother didn't know anything. I went into the kitchen, came up from behind her, picked her up, kissed her, and told her I was leaving. She started weeping. There was an atmosphere of pogrom [mass violence against Jews] in the streets, so I tried to convince Father not to accompany me [to the train station]. I begged but he wouldn't yield. It was night and he accompanied me to the train. I still imagine I hear the echoes of his footsteps. There were few people in the street. This is how I left.[1]

Another Challenge

Through his work in Kowel, Zuckerman proved himself to be an able organizer. In the beginning, he focused on Zionism, recruiting young people to the He-Halutz youth division, known as *Freiheit* ("freedom"), or Dror. He also established training kibbutzim (collective settlements), where students could practice the agricultural skills they would need to work in Palestine.

Yitzhak Zuckerman

Zuckerman's time in Kowel ended when He-Halutz sent him to Warsaw to rebuild Zionist youth programs that had faltered during the German occupation. Zuckerman expected danger, but he soon realized that expecting was a far cry from experiencing:

Those were very hard times for me. I had brought stocks of experiences from a country occupied by the Soviets . . . in their occupation zone [I] walked around like a free person. . . . Here, when I went into the street in the morning with my young comrades, I saw the ruins of Warsaw, and German soldiers hunting Jews.[2]

He also found a group of dedicated workers who were committed to the Jewish people and the Zionist dream. Among that group was Zivia Lubetkin, a young woman who dedicated

Zionism brought Jews from many walks of life together in a common cause: to create a Jewish state in Palestine, the ancient homeland of their people. The movement was the brainchild of Theodor Herzl, an Austrian-Jewish journalist, who made the case for Zionism in his book *The Jewish State* (1896). He based his argument on the history of antisemitism in Europe:

> *We have sincerely tried everywhere to merge with the national communities in which we live, seeking only to preserve the faith of our fathers. It is not permitted us. In vain are we loyal patriots, sometimes superloyal; in vain do we make the same sacrifices of life and property as our fellow citizens; in vain do we strive to enhance the fame of our native lands in the arts and sciences, or her wealth by trade and commerce. In our native lands where we have lived for centuries we are still decried as aliens . . . often by men whose ancestors had not yet come at a time when Jewish sighs had long been heard in the country. . . .*[3]

herself to finding food and other necessities for Warsaw's Jews. Lubetkin and Zuckerman would eventually marry, but, during the war, their commitment to the movement came before their relationship with each other.

The Tragedy of Ponary

The movement was still more dream than reality when a messenger brought devastating news from Vilna, Lithuania. Special killing squads rounded up Vilna's Jews and took them outside the city to the Ponary forest. Using trenches that were made for an oil storage facility that was never completed, they established a killing ground. The Nazis forced a line of Jews to stand up in front of a trench, and shot them so that their bodies would fall into it. When they had filled one trench, they moved on to another. The process continued for days, almost without stopping.

Zuckerman remembered summer vacations at Ponary, staying in a forest cabin, far away from the noise and general busyness of the city. "[T]he news that Ponar [sic] was death sliced through me like a razor. The thought had often been on the tip of my tongue but, for the first time that night, I realized this was total death."[4] For several weeks, he held on to the hope that his parents might have gotten out of Vilna, but in time, the hope dimmed and then vanished altogether.

While Zuckerman was coping with his personal loss, the Judenrat and other community leaders tried to convince the ghetto residents that what had happened to the Jews of Vilna could not happen in Warsaw. They argued that Vilna was a special case. Because it had been under Soviet control, the Nazis might have expected the Jewish community to be riddled through with communists and communist sympathizers. Adolf Hitler himself had long attributed the rise of communism in Russia to "Jewish Bolsheviks" (revolutionaries).

Many Jews accepted this explanation of Ponary because the alternatives were just too hard to believe. They ignored Zuckerman's calls for resistance, largely because they felt powerless to do anything meaningful. Even those who wanted to resist had no idea where to start. Then came the great deportation.

Hinter den
Feindmächten:
der Jude

Many Jews in Warsaw attributed the massacre of Vilna's Jews in Ponary to Hitler's hatred of communism. They believed that what happened in the Soviet zone would not happen in Warsaw. Nazi propaganda, like this poster, often portrayed Jews as conspirators in provoking war and supporting the Allies, including the Soviet Union.

Yitzhak Zuckerman and the Great Deportation

The deportation began with an order for the "resettlement" of Warsaw's Jews. Except for a list of exempted categories, the order applied to all Jews, regardless of age or gender. Within two days, the Germans had deported fifteen thousand people, and Judenrat chairman Adam Czerniakow had committed suicide. Yitzhak Zuckerman attended an emergency meeting in the ghetto, hoping to get various youth groups to put aside their differences and form a resistance force.

When his efforts failed, Zuckerman gave up on uniting the entire underground against the Nazis. He decided to change his tactics by starting with three youth groups that shared a connection to He-Halutz: Dror, Hashomer Hatzair, and Akiva. On July 28, delegates from these groups formed the ZOB. With no plan and no weapons, ZOB members were not ready to fight Germans, but they could track down facts. They began with a name: Treblinka. Some people thought it was just another work camp; others suspected a deadlier purpose.

The Truth About Treblinka

In a sense, both sides were right about Treblinka. There was a work camp by that name, east of Warsaw. In July 1942, the Nazis opened a second camp, which they called Treblinka II. It served one purpose: killing human beings as quickly and efficiently as possible.

This is the train station near the Treblinka II death camp. The ZOB found out about the purpose of Treblinka by sending a man to follow the train route. Trains full of people went into the new camp, but they came back empty.

The underground verified the purpose of Treblinka II by sending a man to follow the train route. At the town of Skolow, the train switched to a brand-new stretch of track. According to a Polish railroad worker, the branch was barely a mile long. The trains were packed full of people when they went into Treblinka but empty when they returned. Nobody had seen supply trains going into the camp, and there was no road for wagons or trucks.

This, along with some other reports, made the situation very clear: The Jews of Warsaw were not being "resettled"—they were being murdered. The ZOB did not have the resources to fight the Nazis, but Zuckerman published warning leaflets and distributed them throughout the ghetto. The message was clear and grim: "Resettlement means Treblinka and Treblinka means death."[5]

Winter 1943

After the great deportation, members of ZOB realized that they did not face a choice between living and dying. The only thing left to them was choosing how they would die. Zuckerman made it clear that he wanted to go down fighting, and he convinced the membership of the ZOB to do the same. The first order of business was obtaining weapons and developing tactics for the next confrontation. Though everyone worked hard, the German "aktion" of January 18, 1943, caught them by surprise.

As commanders of fighting units, Yitzhak Zuckerman and Mordechai Anielewicz had planned to coordinate their operations, but they got cut off from one another as soon as the Germans entered the ghetto. Without contact or communication, each unit was on its own.

While Anielewicz's fighters infiltrated the deportation lines, Zuckerman and his unit set up operations on the top floor of an abandoned apartment building on Zamenhof Street. They planned to operate out of hiding, making quick, deadly strikes and equally quick escapes.

The Confrontation

Zuckerman's unit was ready for the Germans when they came:

> The first gang of four or five Germans that entered the house scattered on the staircase. . . . Our people were hidden—some behind doors and some elsewhere. I was sitting in a room with my gun cocked. We heard the shouts: "Raus! (Get Out!)". . . . The sound echoed in the empty house. It was very tense.
>
> I'll never forget that picture: Zacharia Artstein was sitting in the first room and, as I recall, he was holding a book . . . he sat and read, facing the door. They came in and there he was, sitting and reading a book. It didn't even occur to them to tell us to put our hands up. After they entered our room, he shot them in the back. Then we shot too and the Germans began running away . . . we heard a few of them run into the street. . . .[6]

Before the Germans could regroup, Zuckerman's people made their escape, through the attics and over the roofs, from Zamenhof Street to Muranowska Street. Their first encounter had

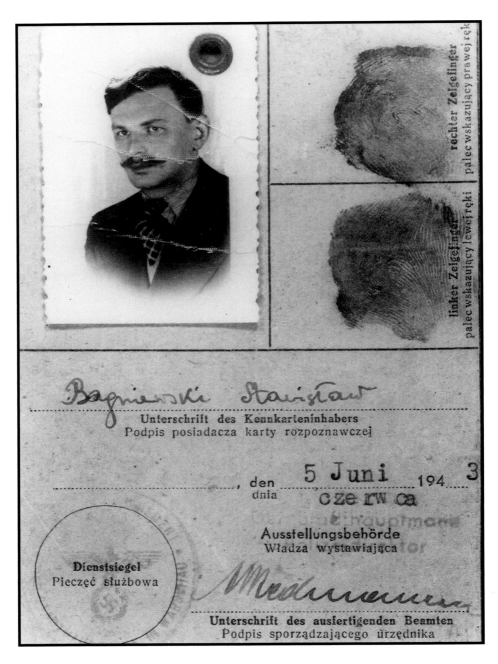

This was Yitzhak Zuckerman's "Aryan" identity card, which gave him a false identity. He needed this ID card in order to carry out operations on the Aryan side of Warsaw.

succeeded beyond expectations. For three more days, the ZOB harried the Germans with surprise attacks in unexpected places.

The January revolt was not a victory for the Jews, but neither was it a crushing loss. ZOB bravery won support from Jews in the ghetto and grudging respect from Polish fighters on the Aryan side—the non-Jewish section of the city, which lay outside the ghetto walls. Zuckerman considered this a major turning point. He summed it up in one sentence: "[The] revolt in January is what made possible the April rebellion."[7]

A Time for Secrets

The ZOB's successes in January put the Germans on high alert. Relying on their network of spies, collaborators, and informants, the Germans kept the underground under careful observation. The ZOB responded by becoming even more secretive than before. The command staff did its battle planning in secret meeting places. Messengers carried vital information to fighting units in the ghetto and operatives on the Aryan side. For an extra layer of security, ZOB operatives used code names. Yitzhak Zuckerman became "Antek."

The name came to stand for Zuckerman's work in the resistance movement. As Antek, he became one of three area commanders in the ghetto. He expected to lead his forces into battle, but that was not to be. When the Germans surrounded the ghetto on April 19, Zuckerman was on the Aryan side of the city, negotiating to buy twenty-eight rifles from the Polish-Communist underground.

Under orders from command headquarters, he remained on the Aryan side, looking for weapons, allies, and information that would help the Jewish cause. This work demanded that he travel in the open, where survival depended upon looking and behaving like an "Aryan." To increase his chances of success, he developed common sense strategies:

I used many restaurants [for meetings], but I wouldn't meet people of different ideological groups in the same restaurant. When making my appointments, I always had to calculate the time it took to walk, because I was afraid to ride the tram [streetcar]. All I had to do was imagine that the tram was suddenly stopped and blocked at both ends, with a [policeman] on every side; but when you walk in the street, you sense the panic sooner and have enough time to hide, to slip into an alley. I had been used to walking for years and it wasn't a problem for me.[8]

Saving the Remnant

By late April, the Germans were burning the ghetto—street by street, one building at a time. Fighters scrambled to keep ahead of the blaze, knowing that they were running out of time and places to hide. On the Aryan side, Zuckerman and his comrades took on a new mission: getting survivors out of the dying ghetto.

The extensive sewer system beneath the city became the escape route of choice. The Jews came through in groups, making their way through a maze of tunnels. On the Aryan side, Zuckerman and his people organized transportation and found hiding places for the refugees.

A man emerges from his hiding place beneath the floor of a bunker built by the ZOB during the Warsaw ghetto uprising. During the final days of the uprising, members of the ZOB tried to save as many Jews as possible using the sewer system as escape routes.

Antek became a rock of stability for the fighters he commanded and the people he helped. As he had done during the fighting, Zuckerman did not let personal feelings interfere with his work. Grief did not stop him when he thought that his girlfriend, Zivia Lubetkin, was dead. And joy did not stop him when he found her alive.

After the liberation of Warsaw in January 1945, Zuckerman gave way to his feelings: "I was thoroughly crushed and broken. . . . [My] struggle for life had a limit. And not only me, everybody. There had always been a sense of mission that gave us strength; but now, it was over. . . . People asked: 'why go on?'"[9]

Zuckerman found his answer to that question in Palestine. In the spring of 1947, he married Zivia Lubetkin, and, together, they helped to build Lohamei Haghetaot, the kibbutz that would become their home. Zuckerman died there on June 17, 1981.

Zivia Lubetkin: Comrade in Arms

Zivia Lubetkin was born on November 9, 1914, into a tightly knit Jewish community in Byden, Poland. Until she started public school, she knew almost nothing about the Gentile world. Though she learned to function within it, she never felt comfortable with its ways. She simply could not think, feel, or behave like a "real" Pole. Perhaps this was partly responsible for her interest in Zionism. As a teenager, she became active in the Zionist-Socialist youth group known as Freiheit, or Freedom (later, Dror).

A Pioneering Spirit

As soon as Lubetkin finished school, she began preparing to become a pioneer in Palestine. This shocked her parents. In Europe in the 1930s, proper young women did not strike out on their own. They remained at home with their parents until they were married. They certainly did not live in unsupervised colonies where men and women mingled freely with one another.

Nobody, including Lubetkin's parents, could change her mind. Without so much as a backward glance, she packed her belongings and headed for a training kibbutz more than a hundred miles from home. Nothing in her upbringing had prepared her for the life she found there—primitive living conditions and hard physical work from sunup to sundown.

After Zivia Lubetkin, pictured here, finished school, she moved to a training kibbutz in preparation for immigration to Palestine.

What Lubetkin lacked in experience she made up in commitment. She immersed herself in training, gladly doing anything from hard labor to the "dirty work" that others tried to avoid. In the process, she transformed herself from a shy village girl into a confident pioneer. The change was so complete that her own family scarcely recognized her:

She was dressed in a leather coat, which was a kind of standard outfit for those undergoing training, and torn and worn-out clothes, and she did not look well. She seemed a different person. Her stories also seemed from another world. She told about her physical work, and how she had "stowed" aboard a train without a ticket, and was caught and arrested. She related how she had spoken before an audience of Jews and Gentiles and how the police came and put her under arrest. Lubetkin was already part of another world, very different than that of her town and contrary to her own home.[1]

The Work in Warsaw

Because of Lubetkin's dedication and her ability to lead by example, the movement called her to its headquarters in Warsaw. She became director of training farms, traveling from place to place, conducting seminars, recruiting members, and raising money for operating expenses. She was doing this work in 1939, when the armies of the Third Reich invaded Poland. Lubetkin and many of her comrades escaped the Nazi onslaught by fleeing to the east, where they were soon living under Soviet control.

The communists could be harsh, and they had little regard for human rights, but they did not slaughter Jews simply for being Jews. This alone made life safer in the Soviet zone. Safety, however, was not Zivia Lubetkin's goal. She wanted to help Jews and promote rebellion against the Nazis. In January 1940, she returned to the Warsaw ghetto and set to work.

She had three goals in Warsaw: reestablish the movement, help the destitute, and organize rebellion against the Nazis. At first, rebellion did not mean taking up arms against a vastly superior force:

. . . [W]hen it seemed to us that German policy was to degrade us and turn us into ignorant slaves, I must admit that even then we did not think that this was total extinction. Thus, our activities in that period—until the news reached us of the concentration camps— focused on the war against the decrees [official orders with the force of law].[2]

A LETTER FROM ZIVIA

Zivia Lubetkin had no patience for those who did not give their best. In this letter to a comrade, she complained about the situation in Kielce, Poland:

March 1935:

Greetings!
I am here in the training farm for a few days already. . . . I must admit that I am a little depressed and I myself don't know why. Was I not aware of reality? The arrangements here are actually quite good, but something is missing, perhaps heart and joy. Each one lives in his own world, with his own interests which are really minor and petty. . . . How I wanted our people to be free, clearly and consciously proud of their way! I have been here for a few days and still feel out of place. . . . Right now, I am sitting in the reading room. It is filled with smoke from the blazing stove, and noise and confusion. People are shouting and joking, and I am sitting with a book open before me but I am not reading it. . . . My heart is aching, and I felt the need to write you.
Yesterday I was in the nearby branch of the movement. I saw terrible poverty and want. . . . Their greatest pleasure is to come pale and starved to the branch and dance the "hora" [a folkdance]. I shall . . . do everything in my power to help them.
As for me, I wanted to study and read, but it is . . . only possible at night but that uses up too much electricity. . . . I came here with the will and energy to act. I hope that the situation will change. I'll be with the group more, and I'll also go out to work and this will certainly encourage me in my work.

Yours,

Zivia[3]

Two young children eat their dinner on the street in the Warsaw ghetto. One of the many things Zivia Lubetkin wanted to do in Warsaw was to help the destitute.

The Great Deportation

The focus changed after German troops invaded the Soviet Union. In Warsaw, Jews began to hear about SS killing squads, but most dismissed the news as rumor. Lubetkin and her comrades were not so quick to judge on the basis of hearsay. Then a traumatized eyewitness reported that these squads were systematically killing the Jews of Vilna.

A year later, it was Warsaw's turn. Beginning on July 22, 1942, Lubetkin watched in horror as Jewish police loaded thousands of people into boxcars. One by one, the trains disappeared and their human "cargo" was never seen again. Exactly one week later, Lubetkin participated in the founding of the ZOB. Not ready to fight, the ZOB warned people to hide or run away instead of reporting to the trains. They also managed symbolic resistance that was both dramatic and satisfying.

Lubetkin and a group of her comrades torched a warehouse filled with property the Germans had stolen from Jews:

We collected mattresses and furniture. . . . Anything inflammable, [and] piled them together and set them on fire. Success! The flames swept into a great blaze and crackled in the night, dancing and twisting in the air. We rejoiced as we saw the reflection of the revenge that was burning inside us, the symbol of the Jewish armed resistance that we had yearned for, for so long.[4]

This moment of rejoicing interrupted the ongoing horror of mass deportations and the grief for the tens of thousands who left Warsaw in freight cars, never to be heard from again. It was almost more than Lubetkin and her comrades could bear:

After the "Aktion" ended and only hundreds instead of thousands of [ZOB] members remained, we met one day and were ashamed to look at each other. Although we knew that the Jewish youth was not guilty for this situation, the fact remained that tens of thousands of Jews went to slaughter while we were still alive. We were ashamed to be alive. At this meeting we all agreed that there was no point in continuing to stay alive and that we must commit suicide collectively. . . . [We] had ten liters of kerosene . . . and two pistols. We proposed going out in the street to burn and kill as many Germans as possible and then die ourselves. . . . But then one person rose and said: "Are we not private individuals and is the real question how will each person put an honorable and decent end to his life? Is not the question how to take advantage of the respite between this 'aktion' which has just ended and the next one which will certainly come in order to prepare for a deed which will be more than the deaths of individuals and which will also save the honor of the survivors?"[5]

The speaker who put an end to plans for suicide was Yitzhak Zuckerman, Lubetkin's comrade in arms and future husband.

The ZOB had to improvise when the Germans unexpectedly began new deportations in January 1943. With no battle plan and no time to make one, the unit commanders improvised a response. Lubetkin commanded a unit of forty men and women: "We fought with grenades, guns, iron rods and light bulbs filled with sulphuric acid," she later noted.[6]

The unit took up a position in an empty apartment building, knowing that the Germans searched every building and every apartment. When jackboots echoed on the wooden stairs, the fighters stood ready. One man shot the first two Germans who burst through the door. The other Germans turned and ran. Lubetkin recorded the encounter in her own words: "For a few minutes we were intoxicated by the thrill of the battle. We had actually witnessed the German conquerors of the world retreat in fright from a handful of young Jews equipped only with a few pistols and hand grenades."[7]

Before the Germans could return with reinforcements, Lubetkin led her unit through musty attics and across snow-covered roofs to a building some five blocks away. They took up positions and waited. When the Germans charged into the entryway, the fighters opened fire and threw a hand grenade. Once more, the Germans retreated, carrying away their dead and wounded. Lubetkin summed up the encounter in one sentence: "Now that we have found the strength to stand up against the murderers, our deaths too would not be in vain."[8]

The Germans pulled out after only four days. Lubetkin took that as a victory:

> The Germans intended to do away with the entire Jewish population of Warsaw this time, but when they were confronted with armed and unexpected opposition, they stopped the "aktion." Evidently it did not seem to them benefiting for Germans to pay with their lives for the death of the Jews of the ghetto.
>
> Now they decided to gain time to achieve this end by finding a new method of annihilation. They did not know that time was also working to our advantage, that in our second confrontation they would have to pay a heavier price.[9]

Days of Death and Fire

The second—and last—confrontation began on April 19. The Germans came at six o'clock in the morning, marching through the main gate and into a ZOB trap. Homemade land mines exploded beneath their feet; grenades, sulfur bombs, and gunfire rained down from the surrounding buildings. German forces retreated, abandoning their dead in the process. Lubetkin's unit saw it all from their station just inside the gate. They knew that this victory was both small and temporary, but still they rejoiced.

Zivia Lubetkin (right) and Yitzhak Zuckerman at their home in Israel after the war. When members of Lubetkin's group thought about committing suicide as their final rebellion, Zuckerman gave a speech convincing them to fight until the end.

As Lubetkin said later: "I cannot tell you which emotion was stronger at the moment, the satisfaction of our revenge or the joy of being alive."[10]

In the following days, ZOB fighters thwarted the Germans time and time again, but each fight weakened them and depleted their small store of arms. It was a matter of time; Lubetkin knew that and so did her comrades. Still, they fought, refusing to yield, even when the Germans torched the ghetto:

> I shall never forget that night when the ghetto was put on fire on all sides. I ran outside from my hiding place, and the night was turned into day. The bright light left me dumbfounded. All around me I heard the crackle of uncontrolled fires, the roar of collapsing houses, and broken glass. Clouds of smoke climbed skyward and the fire spread and consumed everything. . . .
>
> At first, we would slip from house to house through the attics. . . . Now the attics were on fire. We continued to go through the cracks from cellar to cellar, and afterwards we simply wandered through the ruins, avoiding the flames as much as possible. The heat singed our faces and eyes and some people choked on the smoke.[11]

On May 8, the Germans attacked and destroyed the ZOB command center at Mila 18. Lubetkin and two comrades were making their way back to the bunker, expecting to report on their activities. Instead, they found rubble where their headquarters had been. Fourteen comrades lay outside, most so badly injured that they had little chance of survival. Those who could still talk told the story: Mordechai Anielewicz and the rest of the

Jewish resistance fighters are captured by SS troops during the Warsaw ghetto uprising.

command staff had committed suicide rather than be captured by the Germans. They lay buried under the rubble.

Lubetkin later wrote a heartfelt description of that time:

> Our lips muttered words of farewell for our loyal and courageous comrades, the glory of our unhappy heroism. Our hopes and dreams were buried there, all that was most precious to us. We [walked] away stripped, devoid of our dreams, our faith . . . a caravan of bodies moving like spiritless shadows, like ghosts, silent, mourning.[12]

Survivors from the ZOB pose for a photo atop the ruins of Mila 18 after the war on July 1, 1945. Zivia Lubetkin and two comrades came across the ruins of the bunker during the uprising but continued fighting for twenty more days.

The ZOB carried on for twenty more days, fighting and dying in the flames. Lubetkin helped guide survivors out of the ghetto. She traveled from one trouble spot to the next: sometimes living in the city, sometimes in the forests with partisan units, and sometimes in little towns outside of Warsaw. She was staying in one of these little towns on January 17, 1945, when the Russians liberated it.

Many survivors did not know where to go or how to pick up the pieces of their lives. Zivia Lubetkin and her husband, Yitzhak Zuckerman, knew exactly where they wanted to go: Eretz Israel. They achieved this goal after the war and helped to found Kibbutz Lohamei Haghetaot, where they lived together until Zivia's death on July 11, 1978.

5 Simha Rotem: A Man Called Kazik

Simha Rotem was born Shimek Ratheisner in 1925. His parents, Miriam and Zvi Ratheisner, owned and operated a store in a working-class Polish neighborhood. Though they saw to it that Simha received a solid Jewish education, they sent him to a Polish elementary school for his secular studies. Most of his classmates and friends were Gentiles. From them, he learned to speak the everyday Polish of the working class, and developed an easy familiarity with Polish ways.

Not only did Simha behave like a Pole, he looked like one: blond hair, blue eyes, and a "typically Polish" face. He did not make a special effort to blend in with Gentiles; it just happened. At least, it happened until his parents sent him to a Jewish high school. When he was grouped with other Jews, he shared the sting of antisemitism:

> [The] Gentile children used to tease the Jewish children on their way to and from school, so we would walk in a group and felt safer. We didn't run away from Gentile hoodlums but fought back with blows and stones. Once I was attacked with a knife, but somehow it just grazed my head and merely scratched me. Even as a child I was never one to run away.[1]

This is a page from an antisemitic children's book *Der Giftpilz (The Poisonous Mushroom)* published in Germany. Simha Rotem had to deal with antisemitism from Polish children when he attended a Jewish high school.

The Occupation Begins

On September 27, 1939, Warsaw surrendered and the bombings stopped. Simha could never forget watching the victorious Germans march into the city: "The picture is engraved in my memory: perfect order, motorcycles, riders on their horses, steel helmets. I was depressed and scared."[2]

Years later, Simha remembered the early days of German occupation as "more or less bearable." Then came the ghetto and a whole new set of rules. The most immediate problem was food rationing. The Germans used it as a weapon. Adults need an average of 2,550 calories per day. Jews received as little as three hundred calories per person—an allowance that doomed the people of the ghetto to slow starvation.

Simha refused to stand by while Jews starved to death. Over his parents' objections, he joined the growing ranks of ghetto smugglers:

> The illegal trade in food began to flourish right after the Germans introduced rationing. Basic foods became rarities, but you could usually still get them for a high price in the villages. If you managed to smuggle your wares (sausages, potatoes, eggs, cheese) into the city you could make a lot of money. I decided to do something to provide food for my family; I went to the villages several times and brought home

SMUGGLING

This painting by Sophia Kalski, titled "Slice of Bread," depicts her father bringing home a tiny slice of smuggled bread in the Lvov ghetto. Smuggling became a necessity for survival not only in the Warsaw ghetto but in all the ghettos established during the Holocaust.

In the Warsaw ghetto, smuggling was an ordinary part of life. The ZOB did it for weapons and ammunition. The professionals did it for money. Children, as young as six or seven, did it for food.

Simha worked with a network of ZOB couriers, most of them girls and young women, who transported everything from secret documents to weapons and ammunition. The underground chose them because they looked like Gentiles, spoke flawless Polish, and were not afraid to try outrageous methods. For example, one woman went through a German checkpoint with weapons hidden in the bottom of a potato sack. Two others tucked grenades into their underwear and calmly boarded a streetcar on their way back to the ghetto.[3]

Many of the professionals were career criminals who had long experience in evading police. They often focused on high-priced goods rather than necessities, but greed did not always make them disloyal to the Jewish community. For example, the smuggler Shmuel Asher gladly shared his large and luxurious bunker at Mila 18 with the ZOB command staff.

Some child smugglers worked for the professionals, but most supplied their own families with food and medicine. Their work was dangerous but necessary. On German rations alone, a person would starve to death in about three months. By supplying more food, many young smugglers saved the lives of their loved ones.

> enough food to last a few weeks. If you were
> lucky on the train or the road—and if the
> Germans didn't search your bags—you
> succeeded. If you weren't lucky and got
> caught, the food was confiscated and you
> got beaten. Even at this stage, in trips to
> the villages, I looked like a Polish
> Christian. I was fifteen years old and
> looked just like a Gentile.[4]

To the Countryside

Simha's mother and father knew that he was both brave and resourceful, but still they worried. Looking like a Gentile could not protect him from all dangers. The Germans would stop anybody they suspected of smuggling. As a Pole, Simha would be jailed and probably beaten. If the Nazis found out he was Jewish, they might kill him on the spot.

The worried parents wanted their son out of harm's way. They sent him to live with relatives in a small farming village called Klwow, some fifty miles south of Warsaw. There, he found a different world, far from the din of the city and the intrusion of war. Except for occasional Nazi patrols, the Germans left the village alone.

In this peaceful place, Simha found equally peaceful work. A neighboring farmer hired him as a cattle herder. The main part of his job was tending the farmer's cows. It was not hard work.

In the mornings, Simha took the cows to graze in a pleasant meadow. In the afternoons, he took them back to the barn. It was a beautiful time, but somehow Simha never managed to enjoy it: "I was uneasy, haunted by the idea that people in the Ghetto were suffering from hunger and disease while I lay beneath the green grass and the blue sky."[5]

The Kibbutz Training Farm

After about six months, Rotem's conscience drove him back toward Warsaw. He stopped for a time at a Zionist kibbutz outside the city. The newly formed ZOB had taken refuge there, using the kibbutz as a base for operations and combat training. The fighters took an immediate interest in this young Jew, who looked like a Pole, spoke like a Pole, and felt comfortable with Polish ways.

Even before Rotem joined the ZOB, one of the leaders asked him to undertake a mission. It seemed simple enough: Pick up a small package in "Aryan" Warsaw and deliver it to a ZOB operative in the ghetto. Rotem soon learned that his Gentile appearance was a two-edged sword: Getting the package on the Aryan side was not particularly difficult, but delivering it to the ghetto nearly got him captured.

Once, he slipped into line with a work party returning from jobs outside the ghetto. When the Jewish workers saw his blond hair and blue eyes, they whispered among themselves, talking about turning him over to the Germans: "I begged them to believe that I was a Jew and to prove it, I started speaking Yiddish and muttering prayers."[6] When he finally won them over, the Jews

Two young boys are caught smuggling in the Warsaw ghetto. Simha Rotem helped the ZOB by smuggling packages from the Aryan side into the ghetto.

helped get him past the guards. Rotem made his delivery without further incident. Thus began his life as a ZOB freedom fighter.

Becoming Kazik

Not until after the January uprising did Rotem acquire the name that would follow him for the rest of his life. It happened while he and unit commander Hanoch Gutman were trying to get money from the handful of rich Jews still living in the ghetto. The need was so urgent that the ZOB was not above using threats and intimidation to pry loose these supposedly voluntary "contributions."

Rotem never forgot the night when Hanoch Gutman gave him a new identity. The two men were trying to get a wealthy Jew to donate to the cause:

[When he refused] I put the barrel of my revolver near him; he froze and didn't utter a sound. Then Hanoch ordered, "Kazik, kill him!" When he called me Kazik, I was to understand that I had to appear as Kazik, that is, as a Pole. I assumed a strange expression, rolled my eyes, puffed up my chest, grabbed the Jew by the collar and dragged him into a corner of the room. . . . He broke down, asked for a brief delay, went to a hiding place, pulled out some money and reluctantly gave us his "contribution."

Ever since then, the name Kazik has stuck to me.[7]

First Encounters

The uprising began at four o'clock on the morning of April 19. Kazik and a comrade were standing watch in the Brushmaker's area, a neighborhood within the ghetto. From their high balcony,

Simha "Kazik" Rotem

they saw German soldiers,
"walking in an endless procession.
Behind them were tanks, armored
vehicles, light canons, and
hundreds of [SS combat
troops] on motorcycles.
. . . Suddenly I felt how very weak
we were. What force did we have
against an army, against tanks and
armored vehicles? We had nothing but pistols and grenades."[8]

The fighters did have one "super weapon": a large land mine,
buried just inside the Brushmaker's gate. Kazik waited until the
Germans were inside. Then he pushed the alarm button and
grabbed the fuse that would set off the bomb:

At that moment my commander, Hanoch,
burst in, snatched the fuse out of my hand,
and . . . exploded the mine. I was nailed to the
spot, almost paralyzed—a tremendous
explosion! I [wanted] to see it with my own
eyes. And I did see: crushed bodies of soldiers
. . . cobblestones and fences crumbling,
complete chaos. I saw and I didn't believe:
German soldiers screaming in panicky flight,
leaving their wounded behind.[9]

Into the Sewers

For the first few days, the fighters kept the enemy off balance. Then on April 25, the Germans began setting fires. Building by building, the ghetto burned. Kazik later noted that fire "rampag[ed] through every house in the Ghetto. . . . [It] was night, but the flames made it bright as day. Everything all around was on fire, walls were crashing down. We had to go through burning shops, with flames surrounding us on all sides. The heat was unbearable. Slivers of glass in the yards were melted."[10]

As the ghetto burned, ZOB survivors began looking for escape routes. They eventually decided to go through the sewer system. To do that, they needed a guide—someone who knew the way through that vast maze of interconnecting tunnels.

German soldiers walk through the streets of the Warsaw ghetto as residential buildings burn to the ground. As the ghetto went up in flames, Kazik and other surviving members of the ZOB worked to help Jews escape through the underground sewers.

Ryszek Musselman, a communist with contacts on the Aryan side, approached two sewer workers with a concocted story about rescuing Polish underground fighters who had been trapped in the ghetto. On May 8, Kazik, Musselman, and the two sewer workers descended into the tunnels:

It was ten o'clock at night and pitch-dark in the sewers, where there was neither day nor night. . . . We started walking: the sewer workers first, with me behind. . . . The guides changed their mind from time to time and threatened to desert us. I gave them drinks; sometimes I cajoled them and sometimes I browbeat them and threatened them with my gun—and thus we advanced. At a certain moment the two men said, "That's it, we're inside the Ghetto." I climbed the iron ladder in the wall of the sewer. Ryszek stayed below to keep the guides from taking off. I lifted the manhole cover and found that we really were in the Ghetto. . . . It was two o'clock in the morning.[11]

While Ryszek and the sewer workers waited below, Kazik went to find survivors to bring out of the ghetto. He found only death: ashes, corpses, burned-out buildings. A question pressed on his mind: Was there anybody left to rescue? He found the answer to that question in the sewer. A small group of fighters came out of a side tunnel, filthy and frightened but very much alive. Other survivors hid in bunkers and basements within the ghetto.

Kazik sent two of the new arrivals to find this second group, while the rest waited for transportation. Two "Polish-looking" fighters had already gone to get a truck. As soon as it came, survivors began crawling out of the sewer and climbing into the truck. When curious onlookers stopped to watch, Kazik knew that the SS would not be far behind.

As soon as the last fighters had boarded the truck, he gave the order to leave. Zivia Lubetkin insisted on waiting for the second group. When Kazik refused, she drew her gun and threatened to shoot him. "No problem," [Kazik] said. "We will soon finish the matter in the forest: You will shoot me and I will shoot you."[12]

Lubetkin backed down, and the truck left. Kazik soon learned the cost of his decision. The second group fell into the hands of the Gestapo. None of them survived. This was just one of the painful memories that followed Kazik when he tried to rebuild his life after the war.

He went to Palestine in June 1946, only to realize that adjusting to this new life would not be easy. He had to learn contemporary Hebrew, get a job, and find a place to live. He also had to come to terms with the past. This did not mean forgetting his days as Kazik, the freedom fighter. But it did mean remembering how to be Simha Rotem, son of Miriam and Zvi Ratheisner, free citizen of Israel.

Vladka Meed: Underground Courier

Vladka Meed was born Feigele Peltel in Warsaw on December 29, 1921. She grew up speaking Yiddish, the folk language of East European Jewry. Her parents, Shlomo and Hanna Peltel, were staunch anti-Zionists, who wanted to create a secular Jewish community somewhere in Europe. It would be based on the Yiddish language and culture of Jews in Poland and other east European nations.

Feigele grew up speaking Yiddish at home and at school. When she was old enough, she joined *Zukunft* ("future" in Yiddish). The group was more cultural than political. Its members attended the Yiddish theater, held seminars on Yiddish literature, and participated in various projects that advanced the Yiddish language and community.

Unlike many members of Zukunft, Feigele could speak Polish without an accent. She had learned from her sister, who attended a Polish public school. Until the Germans came, she had no idea how important that would be.

The Time of Quiet Resistance

In the beginning, German occupational authorities tried to control the Jewish community by attacking its way of life. They banned religious, educational, and cultural activities, only to

A group of children in kindergarten line up outside their school six months prior to the establishment of the Warsaw ghetto. Once the ghetto was established, all Jewish schools were closed. However, teachers created secret schools throughout the ghetto.

find that the Jews of Warsaw were determined to keep their traditions alive. Teachers created secret schools for children. Rabbis held Sabbath services in basements, abandoned shops, and anywhere else they could find some measure of safety. Political groups gathered to discuss pressing issues, journalists produced underground newspapers, and scholars gave lectures.

Like her comrades in Zukunft, Feigele became an enthusiastic participant in these underground activities. One of her few pleasant memories of that time concerned one particular lecture:

> *[It was] held on a cold winter's evening in 1941 in one of the soup kitchens: We were a group of youngsters, 15-16 years old, huddled together for warmth, and despite the hunger that gnawed at each of us, we listened to the leader speak about the writer Y. L. Peretz. Later we had to spread out to various houses, to talk on the same subject. My assignment was on No. 30 Pawia St. I managed to get there before the curfew. I remember the large room, in which 40 occupants of the house had gathered. The windows were blacked out. A guard had been stationed outside the room, in case of a surprise "visit" by the Germans. My talk was on the Peretz story "Bontshe Shveig." I do not recall the discussion, but I can never forget the wonderful atmosphere, the feeling of being able, even for a short time, to get away from the bitter ghetto reality.[1]*

As time passed, getting away from the oppressive realities of ghetto life became more and more difficult. People died of typhus and starvation. Some were shot down in the streets for no particular reason, and some took their own lives. In spite of all this, most Jews clung to the hope of personal survival for themselves and their loved ones. They believed that violence against the Germans would only endanger this survival. Looking back on those days, Feigele explained:

> *Acts of violence against the Germans—prior to the uprising—were not committed because we in the ghetto did not believe that such acts would serve our purpose. The Germans enforced a diabolical method of collective responsibility: for every German killed by a Jew, hundreds of Jews would be killed. Our aim was to survive, to live, to outwit the enemy and witness his destruction. Every effort that lent strength to this goal, I see as an act of resistance.[2]*

For a time, following German rules when necessary and breaking them whenever possible seemed to be working. Then came the great deportation, and everything changed.

The Deportation Notice

On July 22, 1942, the Germans posted notices all over the ghetto, announcing that " . . . all the Jews of Warsaw, regardless of age or sex, will be deported."[3] A list of exempt categories followed, including Jews who worked for German firms.

Like others who were not on the short list of exemptions, Feigele searched frantically for a job that would give her an

Der Judenrat in Warschau

Im Auftrage des Arbeitsamtes — Warschau gibt der Judenrat folgendes bekannt:

ARBEITSAMT WARSCHAU
Nebenst   für den Jüd. Wohnbezirk

ANORDNUNG.

„Ein Wechsel des Arbeitsplatzes darf nur mit vorheriger Genehmigung des Arbeitsamtes Warschau, Nebenstelle für den jüd. Wohnbezirk erfolgen.

...seine Arbeitsstelle verlässt wird sofort ausgesiedelt".

Arbeitsamt Warschau

Warschau, den .   12.

gez. ZIEGLER, Regierungsinspektor

Rada Żydowska w Warszawie

Warszawa, dn. 25 sierpnia 1942

Z polecenia Urzędu Pracy Warszawa Rada Żydowska podaje do wiadomości:

URZĄD PRACY WARSZAWA
Oddział dla Dzielnicy Żydowskiej

ZARZĄDZENIE

„Zmiana miejsca pracy może nastąpić jedynie za uprzednim zezwoleniem Urzędu Pracy Warszawa, Oddział dla dzielnicy żydowskiej.

Kto opuści swoje miejsce pracy, zostanie natychmiast wysiedlony".

Urząd Pracy Warszawa

(—) ZIEGLER, Regierungsinspektor

Warszawa, dnia 24.8.1942 r.

Umsiedlungsdruckerei Gericht r. 24.

Beginning in July 1942, only Jews with an employment card were exempt from "resettlement." This decree notice issued by the Jewish Council on August 24, 1942, announces that people who change jobs must receive permission from the employment office or they will be deported from Warsaw.

employment card. The best she could get was a "small scribbled note" that authorized her to register at Toebbens' workshop, one of the largest employers in the ghetto.

That was not much, but it was all she had when she faced her first "selection." This process was both humiliating and terrifying. Jews had to line up and pass before German officers, who sorted them into two groups: one to the right, one to the left. Those sent to the right would live. Those sent to the left were loaded onto wagons and taken to the railway depot.

Feigele moved slowly ahead in the line, until she faced the German inspector who would decide her fate:

> [He] took the note and held it for a moment. With a skeptical glance at me, he asked . . . "Is this your employment card?"
>
> "Yes," I muttered, "it's my employment card from Toebbens." I had anticipated his verdict and now was impatient to have done with it. The inspector threw me another piercing look.
>
> "To the right!"[4]

Stunned, Feigele followed a Jewish policeman to the "safe" side of the street and took her place among the survivors. They stood with blank faces and haunted eyes, watching as Jewish police and Gentile guards loaded deportees into the wagons.

Feigele Peltel pictured on a mission for the Jewish underground in 1944.

Feigele would never see her mother and brother again. Her father had died of pneumonia a year earlier. Later, when the Germans took her sister, Feigele became the last surviving member of her family. She was just twenty years old.

BREAD AND MARMALADE

The Germans knew how to manipulate people to act against their own best interests. One of these tricks cost the lives of Vladka Meed's mother and brother: "The Germans were giving before the entry to the trains, bread and marmalade for the people to make them believe that they are going to be resettled into other cities when the truth was that they were being taken to Treblinka, to the gas chambers."

To ensure success, the Germans actually gave three kilograms (6.6 pounds) of bread and one kilogram (2.2 pounds) of marmalade to each volunteer. The prospect of food drew Meed's mother and little brother to the trains. Part of her wanted to go with them, though she knew the train's true destination: " . . . somehow I couldn't decide and I couldn't make myself go. . . . Even today it bothers me."[5]

A New Task

The great deportation turned the once-bustling ghetto into a ghost town of empty buildings and empty streets. Amid the desolation, young Jews talked about fighting back, whatever the consequences. Feigele noted that "a spark had been smoldering even during the 'peaceful' days of the ghetto. Now it began to glow, slowly, tentatively at first, then ever more fiercely."[6]

Not until October did this "spark" convince the anti-Zionist Bund and its youth groups to join the ZOB. The Bund was a socialist organization that wanted to build secular (non-religious) Jewish communities, based upon the language and culture of Eastern European Jewry. It was a big gap to cross, but Bundist leader Abrasha Blum managed to do it.

He called an urgent meeting to announce the agreement and hand out assignments. One by one, each person became responsible for building a fighting unit at a specific location within the ghetto. For Feigele, he had a different mission. With her Gentile looks and perfect Polish, she would cross to the Aryan side. "You'll get your instructions in a few days' time," he told her, and with that, the conversation ended.[7]

Days turned into weeks, but the promised instructions finally came. She would be leaving the ghetto within two days.

In "Aryan" Warsaw

Feigele Peltel got out of the ghetto by slipping into line with a work crew, bound for the Aryan side. She had her "Aryan" looks, her unaccented Polish, and false identity papers for Wladyslawa

(Vladka) Kowalska (later Meed). She now had a new name. Her job included making contacts with friendly Gentiles, helping Jews in hiding, and getting weapons whenever and wherever she could find them. She also acted as a courier, shuttling supplies and information between the ghetto and the outside world.

On one mission, Meed nearly got caught with ten pounds of dynamite. She picked it up on the Aryan side and went to a prearranged place, where Polish smugglers set up a ladder against the ghetto wall:

As I reached the top, shots rang out from the street. A German patrol was approaching. In an instant, the smugglers snatched the ladder away and took cover. There I was, sitting on top of the wall, holding my parcel. The ghetto wall was over 3 meters [10 feet] high. I was afraid to jump because the explosives might go off. The shooting came closer and I was sure that my time had come. Just then, I heard shouts from the Jewish side of the wall: "Wait, we'll help you." Three of my ghetto friends came running to the wall. They had watched me from their hiding place. In a moment they had formed a human ladder, snatched my bundle, and helped me descend. In no time we ran away from the wall.[8]

Document fields (identity card):

Kennort / Miejsce wystawienia: W[...]

Kreish. / tarostwo powiat. — Distrikt / Okręg: Warschau

Kennummer / Numer rozpoznawczy: 657218

Gültig bis / Ważne do: 9 Oktober 1948 / października

Name / Nazwisko: Wąchalska

Geburtsname (b. Ehefrau) / Nazwisko panieńskie (u mężatek)

Vorname / Imię: Stanisława Maria

Geboren am / Urodzony (a) w dn.: 10.4.1919

Geburtsort / Miejsce urodzenia: Warschau

Kreish. / Starostwo pow.: Warschau — Distrikt / Okręg: Warschau

Land / Kraj:

Beruf / Zawód: erlernter / wyuczony: Buchhalterin . buchalterka
ausgeübter / wykonywany: Buchhalterin buchalterka

Religion / Wyznanie: röm.kath. rzym.kat.

Besondere Kennzeichen / szczególne znaki rozpoznawcze: keine nie ma

Unterschrift des Kennkarteninhabers / Podpis posiadacza karty rozpoznawczej: Wąchalska Stanisława

Warschau, den 9 Oktober 19[...] / dnia października

Dienstsiegel / Pieczęć służbowa

Ausstellungsbehörde / Władza wystawiająca

Unterschrift des ausfertigenden Beamten / Podpis sporządzającego urzędnika

Witness to the Unthinkable

Meed did not allow her experience on the wall to make her fearful or cautious. She did what had to be done, performing her duties with little thought of personal danger. Despite the hard work of Meed and others in the ZOB, the January aktion came as a surprise. Only a few fighters had weapons, but they fought until they ran out of ammunition, causing many casualties.

The bravery of the ZOB fighters turned the tide of public opinion. The majority of the remaining ghetto residents supported the ZOB and taking steps to protect themselves when the Germans returned. Meed saw the difference every time she entered the ghetto:

Feigele Peltel received this false identity card, which gave her a new name: Wladyslawa (Vladka) Kowalska. She eventually became Vladka Meed after marriage.

On my missions, I could hear the sounds of hammering; Jews were secretly building bunkers and hiding places. Shots rang out; young people were learning to handle firearms. The whole ghetto was preparing to face a new deportation. . . . None of them expected to survive a Nazi attack. Nor did we expect to influence, in the smallest way, the outcome of the war. But we were fuelled by the conviction that the enemy must be fought.[9]

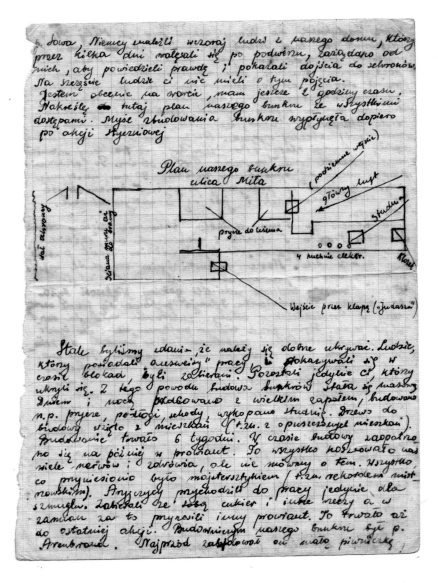

This photo of a diary page shows a diagram of a hideout and a description in Polish by a Jewish woman of her final days during the Warsaw ghetto uprising. The six-page diary was written by an unnamed woman and was released on December 7, 2004, by the Ghetto Fighters' House in northern Israel. Vladka Meed saw these hideouts being built when she entered the ghetto delivering valuable packages to her comrades.

When German troops surrounded the ghetto in April, Meed and her comrades, who were outside the ghetto walls, knew that the battle had begun. They swung into action, smuggling arms, ammunition, and information to their comrades in the ghetto. Meed and others tried to get weapons from the Polish underground, only to be told "to hold on a little longer."[10]

On the sixth day of fighting, German dive-bombers launched a deadly rain of incendiary (fire-starting) bombs on the ghetto. Then foot soldiers entered and systematically torched every building left standing. As the ghetto burned, Vladka Meed and her comrades could do nothing but watch: "We stared into the

Three Jewish partisans stand in the Wyszkow forest near Warsaw. Vladka Meed helped the partisans living in the forest by bringing them much-needed supplies.

fiery sky over Warsaw. Why was there no response from the rest of the city? Where was the help our neighbors had promised? And the rest of the world—why was it so silent?"[11]

After the uprising, Vladka Meed kept working to save Jewish lives. She got false papers for Jews who could pass as Gentiles and found hiding places for those who could not pass. When surviving fighters set up camp in the forest, she became their lifeline for supplies and information.

During this time, she worked with Benjamin Meed, who shared her dedication to the hidden Jews and her determination to tell the world about the uprising. The two married in 1945 and eventually made their way to the United States.

In the years that followed, they built a good life. They had two children, both of whom became doctors. In 1981, they founded the Benjamin and Valdka Meed Registry of Jewish Holocaust Survivors at the United States Holocaust Memorial Museum in Washington, D.C. Amid the satisfactions of their life, Vladka Meed learned to live with her memories, but she never found an answer to the questions she had asked while the ghetto burned: Where was the rest of the world, and why was it silent?

Facts about Marek Edelman's childhood and family background are difficult to find. He was born in 1919, 1921, or 1922, in Poland or in neighboring Belarus. He had little memory of his father, who died when he was very young. His mother was a socialist, who supported Yiddish culture, but rejected both Zionism and Jewish religious practices. She died when her son was thirteen, leaving him alone in the world.

Marek proved to be intelligent and resourceful. With occasional help from his late mother's coworkers, he got along nicely, living on his own. In the process, he developed a maturity beyond his years. That would hold him in good stead when the Germans invaded his homeland.

When the occupational authorities appointed a Jewish council under the leadership of Adam Czerniakow, many hoped that this would mean a degree of self-government for Warsaw's Jewish community.

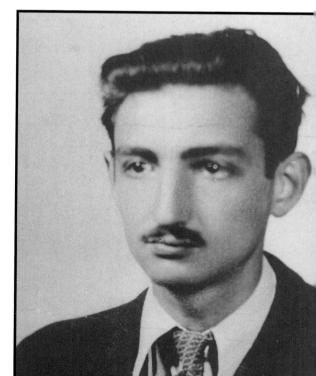

Marek Edelman

Into the Ghetto

Marek Edelman did not share this hope. As events developed around him, he saw increasing signs of a dark future:

> There was only one punishment for failure to obey regulations—death. . . . To top it all, the unwritten law of common responsibility was . . . applied against the Jews. . . . [For example] 53 male inhabitants of the 9 Nalewki Street apartment house were . . . shot for the beating of a Polish policeman by one of the tenants. This occurrence, the first case of mass punishment, intensified the feeling of panic amongst the Warsaw Jews.[1]

Fear grew and spread. A year after the Nalewki killings, the Germans set up the ghetto and forced Jews to move into the area. When they had completed the roundup, they started building walls. Marek Edelman watched those walls grow, brick upon brick, isolating the ghetto from the rest of the city:

> The complete segregation of the Ghetto, the regulations under which no newspaper could be brought into it, and all the news from the outside world carefully kept out, had a very definite purpose. These

> *regulations contributed to the development of a special way of thinking common to the Ghetto inhabitants. Everything taking place outside the Ghetto walls became more and more foggy, distant, strange. Only the present day really mattered. . . .*[2]

An Omen of Things to Come

In the spring of 1942, Edelman began to realize that each "present day" would be more deadly than the one before it. A new round of killings began on the night of April 17, when the Germans dragged over fifty social workers from their homes and shot them in the street. Nobody knew why. As Edelman wrote later: "Some concluded that the aktion was aimed at editors of clandestine papers, and that all illegal activities should have been stopped so as not to needlessly increase the tremendous number of victims."[3]

Edelman realized that "illegal activities" had little to do with the killings. The Nazis were not killing Jews because of anything they did or did not do. They were killing Jews simply because they were Jews.

After the social workers, random killings increased at an alarming rate. According to Edelman, the Nazis "killed between ten and fifteen Jews every night. Nobody could predict when the next attack would come, or who would be its target." According to Edelman, victims came "from all social groups—smugglers, merchants, workers, professionals, etc." The purpose was "to

A view inside a workshop in the Warsaw ghetto. Trapped behind the ghetto walls, Jews were forced to work for the Nazis and occasionally received food for their labor.

paralyse [*sic*] even the smallest acts of . . . resistance and to force . . . blind, passive subordination from the Jews."[4]

The Man at the Gate

The Germans did not stop with fear. They also turned hope into a weapon of control. While they were deporting people by the thousands, they handed out hundreds of "life tickets," exempting broad classes of people from deportation. The categories included hospital patients and others who were too sick for work.

Because Edelman was a messenger for the ghetto hospital, he was assigned to decide who was sick enough to qualify for this exemption. He stood at the gate of the Umschlagplatz to select people sick enough to stay. His top priority was to choose perfectly healthy ZOB leaders:

> *I was merciless. One woman begged me to pull out her fourteen-year-old daughter, but I was only able to take one more person and I took Zosia, who was our best courier. . . . At the beginning it was the people without life tickets [work cards] who paraded past me. . . . But later, they were even taking those with tickets.*[5]

A Jewish woman appears in a photo taken during a deportation from the Warsaw ghetto. Marek Edelman stood at the gate of the Umschlagplatz to hand out "life tickets," which allowed people to stay in the ghetto. It was a very difficult job, as Edelman often had to refuse the pleas of mothers to save their children.

Later still, the Germans entered the hospital and killed the sick people they had once spared. After the slaughter came the great deportation, and Edelman was among the first to call for open resistance. After much soul-searching and talk of mass suicide, the underground decided to make a fight of it.

In Desperate Battle

On April 19, 1943, Edelman woke to the sound of gunfire:

[B]ecause of the chilly morning and the fact that the firing seemed to come from far off, I found no reason to get up. It was not until the next day, April 20, that the Germans penetrated our area. They advanced towards the gate of the brush-making factory, where we had placed a mine [a buried bomb]. At the very moment when the Germans reached the gate we sprang the mine. Over one hundred SS soldiers were blown up and the Germans who survived were fired at by the partisans. It is a great triumph to us. Later that evening three SS soldiers with lowered tommy guns and white armlets appeared in the ghetto. They wanted to negotiate with us, and proposed a 15-minute truce to remove the dead and the wounded and promised all inhabitants an orderly *evacuation to labor if they surrendered. Our answer was firing. We fired with our sole machine-gun. Certainly we missed. But that was less important. The important thing was that we showed the world that we shot.*[6]

An interviewer once asked Edelman why shooting was so important. His answer was brief and to the point: "Humanity had decided that dying with a gun is more beautiful than dying without a gun. So we went along with this decision."[7]

A Jewish fighter surrenders his weapon to German soldiers after being captured during the uprising.

What the fighters lacked in experience they made up for in reckless bravery. Edelman remembered running over rooftops and shooting and standing at a high window, flinging homemade bottle bombs into the street below:

> I was able to do a lot of things then. To lose five men in a battle and not feel guilty. To nod off to sleep while the Germans were drilling holes in order to blow us up (I simply knew that there was nothing more to be done at the moment); and . . . when they'd break for lunch at noon, we'd quickly do what was necessary to get out. . . . I was capable of telling a guy who'd asked me to give him the address of a contact on the Aryan side: "not yet, it's too early." . . . [He said] "there must be some place over there I can get to. . . ." Was I supposed to tell him that there was no such [address]? So I told him: "It is too early yet."[8]

Though Edelman had faced the grim realities ahead, he saw no reason to destroy somebody else's last shreds of hope. Circumstances would do that soon enough. In his determination to face reality, Edelman refused to glorify the uprising, or his own role in it.

When Mordechai Anielewicz died in Mila 18, Edelman was his deputy. With little discussion and no fanfare, he assumed command over the last desperate days of the resistance. The end, when it came, was what he had expected it to be: the complete destruction of the Warsaw ghetto. A tiny remnant of the ZOB escaped its charred remains, some to find shelter on the Aryan side, others to hide in the nearby forest.

The Truth According to Marek Edelman

When the war ended in 1945, Zionists headed for Palestine to begin creating a new Jewish state. True to his Bundist philosophy, Marek Edelman did not go to Palestine. He chose to remain in Poland, where he became a prominent cardiologist (heart doctor) and a tireless advocate for human rights.

Right after the war, he wrote a short book about his experiences. After that, he rarely talked about the uprising, and, when he did, he downplayed its significance: "There were only two hundred and twenty of us. . . . Can you even call that an uprising? All it was about, finally, was that we would not just let them slaughter us when our turn came. It was only a choice as to the manner of dying."[9]

In 1968, political struggles triggered a new wave of antisemitism in Poland. Edelman became one of many Jews who lost his job and his position in the community. Many left the country, but Edelman rode out the crisis and eventually got a new job in his field.

In this photo, a large group of people run away from Warsaw University as police attack student rioters. The 1968 riots ended in Poland with an antisemitic campaign by the communist regime that drove fifteen thousand Jews out of Poland. Despite the violent attacks and losing his job, Marek Edelman remained in Poland and lived there until his death.

YELLOW FLOWERS

Though Marek Edelman downplayed both the uprising and his own role as the ZOB's last commander, somebody chose to remember for him. Every year on April 19, an anonymous person marked the anniversary of the uprising with a bunch of yellow flowers. A delivery boy would bring them to Edelman's door, then leave without saying a word.

The flowers came every year, with just one exception: 1968, when antisemitism once more endangered Poland's Jewish population. When the confrontation passed, the deliveries resumed and continued at least into the late 1970s. There is no further mention of them after that.

Edelman never found out who sent the flowers, why they were always yellow, or why he was chosen to receive them: "Certainly I do not expect any flowers. . . . They just keep coming. But that year when I did not get any flowers, I felt melancholic. It made me sad."[10]

After his experience, Edelman had few illusions about life. When an interviewer asked what he considered most important in life, his answer was characteristically modest and undramatic: "Basically, it is life itself that is most important. And if there is life, then most important is freedom. And then one gives one's life for freedom. It is hard to say what is most important after that."[11]

Marek Edelman died on October 2, 2009, at the approximate age of ninety.

8 General Jurgen Stroop: The Executioner

urgen Stroop was born Josef Stroop on September 26, 1895, in Detmold, Germany. His father, Konrad, was chief of police for the principality (territory) of Lippe-Detmold. Though the position brought neither wealth nor social standing, the Stroops did live close to Detmold Castle, home of Lippe's aristocratic rulers.

The boy grew up with a near-reverence for the power, status, and wealth that the castle represented. The quest for these things would shape the rest of his life: "Right sides with power," he once said, "and power is backed by God."[1] He learned what was "right" from his parents and other authority figures. He also learned not to ask questions and not to disobey orders.

In the Stroop household, all forms of misbehavior had immediate consequences. Even as an adult, Stroop could remember scoldings and beatings, but he never rebelled against his parents. He tried to appease them by strict obedience to every rule. By the time he became an adult, he had learned to do as he was told, think what authority figures told him to think, and believe what they told him to believe.

The Way of a Soldier

Stroop's ability to follow orders made him ideally suited for the military. He joined the German army on August 18, 1914, shortly after the outbreak of World War I. By mid-September, he was on the western front, seeing France for the first time. He loved the land, but he despised the people as "a nation of half-castes and anarchists."[2]

He did not stay among them for very long. In October, he was wounded and taken to a hospital behind the lines. During his recovery, he was able to visit his hometown, where people who once ignored him hailed him as a hero. On December 2, 1915, he received the Iron Cross Second Class for his service in France: "The day they pinned that medal on my chest, I felt like I was in a Germanic heaven."[3]

That "heaven" ended with the war, and Stroop returned to Detmold with his medals and his memories. It was then that he learned that neither the memories nor the medals had any practical value. Though he dreamed of becoming an officer, he left the service as an enlisted man. Back in Detmold, he ended up with a low-paying job in the Land Registry office. He lacked the education and social connections to aspire to anything more.

Rising Through the Ranks

In the 1920s, Stroop discovered a new movement that offered opportunity to people stuck on the lower rungs of German society. Its leader, Adolf Hitler, was an enlisted man whose formal schooling ended at the eighth grade. Despite these humble circumstances, Hitler talked about an "Aryan" master race that would cleanse Germany of Jews, communists, political liberals, and others who had no place in the New Order. Stroop, who

Jurgen Stroop (center) watches housing blocks burn during the suppression of the Warsaw ghetto uprising. Stroop joined the German army on August 18, 1914, after the outbreak of World War I.

had long believed that Germans were superior to other peoples, responded to the call in 1932 by joining both the Nazi Party and the SS.

Having taken this step, Stroop set out to create a near-perfect Nazi image for himself. He learned to think, talk, and behave like a Nazi: embracing racism and antisemitism, strutting about in shined riding boots, carrying a whip, and treating "lesser" people with undisguised contempt.

As he made his way up the promotions ladder, Stroop found his given Christian name to be something of an embarrassment.

"Joseph" came from his devout Catholic mother. It had served well enough in his early years, but a biblical name was entirely unsuitable for an officer in the SS:

> . . . [W]e Nazis, particularly those of us in the SS, were anti-Catholic and opposed to all types of Judeo-Christian influence. Difficult though it was, we tried to restore the old ways and institutions, including the traditional Germanic names. I couldn't stand the name Joseph. It struck me as the opposite of everything Nordic. . . . I spoke to the personnel people at SS headquarters about taking the name Jurgen. . . . I explained that I wanted a name that reflected [Nazi] ideology and pointed out that Jurgen had been the name of my dead son. . . . (Jurgen, Stroop's firstborn child, died in infancy).[4]

These outward signs of loyalty got him noticed in Berlin, but it was his ability to follow orders without question that got him promoted. In March 1934, the policeman's son from Detmold finally became an officer: a captain in the SS. He went on to command several SS units in Germany and fight on the Russian front in the summer of 1941. Along the way, he received promotions and decorations. By the time he was assigned to the Warsaw ghetto in 1943, he was an SS general.

Assignment Warsaw

When Stroop arrived in Warsaw, plans for the first assault were completed, with Colonel Ferdinand von Sammern-Frankenegg in command. Stroop began hatching plots to get rid of von Sammern, only to find that he did not need them. This son of the aristocracy managed to discredit himself with the first assault on April 19, 1943.

While Stroop was in prison, awaiting trial for his role in destroying the Warsaw ghetto, he told his cellmates the story:

> It was clear from the first that [von Sammern] had entered the ghetto . . . with insufficient forces—only eight hundred and fifty men, including sixteen officers. There wasn't a sound for the first five minutes. Then, just as von Sammern was probably thinking that his SS men would stroll through the Ghetto like tourists, the shooting began. Our troops started to panic under the strong, well-aimed fire, but von Sammern's officers somehow managed to keep them advancing in tight formation. Suddenly . . . a mine exploded, wounding several of our people. Those Jews weren't just resisting . . . they attacked us.[5]

Nazi soldiers pause to eat a meal during the Warsaw ghetto uprising. When General Stroop arrived in Warsaw, he quickly took control of the operation.

Stroop continued to recite von Sammern's blunders, such as deploying two armored cars and a tank into streets so narrow that they could barely move. When the Jewish fighters put them out of commission with Molotov cocktails, the Germans had no choice but to retreat.

After the morning debacle, Heinrich Himmler, *Reichsführer* (Reich Leader) of the SS, relieved von Sammern of his duties and told Stroop to lead a new attack in two hours. By breaking the attack force into small groups, Stroop hoped to reduce the overall damage to his forces. This hasty operation was good enough to get what Stroop wanted: full command of German forces in Warsaw.

Stroop's "War"

Under Stroop, the Germans picked apart the resistance one attic, basement, and underground bunker at a time. Stroop reported every operation in detail. In one report he praised

the men of the Waffen-SS [SS combat troops], the Police, and Wehrmacht [regular army] who tirelessly fulfilled their duties in true comradeship and stood together as exemplary soldiers. Their mission often lasted from early morning to late at night. Nightly search patrols . . . dogged the Jews and gave them no respite. Jews who used the night to supplement their provisions from abandoned bunkers and to make contact or exchange news with neighboring groups were often brought to bay and finished off.

Considering that the greater part of the men of the Waffen-SS had been trained for only 3 or 4 weeks before this operation, they must be given special recognition for their daring, courage, and devotion to duty. It must be noted that the Wehrmacht Engineers also executed their tasks of blowing up bunkers, sewers, and concrete houses with tireless devotion. The officers and men of the Police . . . acquitted themselves with devil-may-care valor.[6]

General Stroop (center) and other SS soldiers search the entrance
to an underground bunker during the Warsaw ghetto uprising.

Stroop's choice of words not only dramatized events but also offered glimpses into his character. To him, the SS troops who slaughtered Jews were daring and courageous. The engineers who blew up bunkers, buildings, and sewer tunnels acted with "tireless devotion."[7]

By contrast, Stroop described the Jewish fighters and their exploits with open contempt.

For example, his report for May 8 described the ZOB fighters as "subhumans" and "creatures" that were "liquidated" or "destroyed" by the SS.[8] He did not allow them enough humanity to say that they were "killed."

In this same report, Stroop detailed the German assault on the ZOB command bunker at Mila 18. For some reason, he chose not to dramatize this important event, sticking mainly with facts and figures: "We succeeded in opening the bunker of the party leadership and seizing about 60 heavily armed bandits. . . . About 200 Jews were sheltered in this bunker; 60 of them were apprehended and 140 destroyed due to the strong impact of smoke candles and heavy explosives laid in several places."[9]

After the assault on Mila 18, Stroop knew that the end was in sight. Most of the leaders were dead and most of the ammunition was gone. By mid-May, he was ready to declare victory, but he wanted to do it "in a suitably artistic manner."[10]

When he had given the matter some thought, Stroop decided to blow up Warsaw's largest and most beautiful synagogue. He told the story to his cellmates with great enthusiasm:

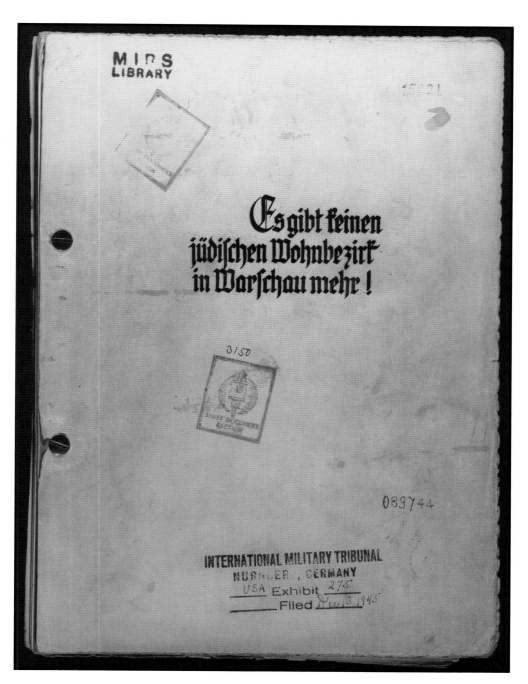

**Es gibt keinen
jüdischen Wohnbezirk
in Warschau mehr!**

0/50

089744

A copy of the cover page of the Stroop Report, entitled, "The Jewish Quarter of Warsaw is no more!"

> *What a marvelous sight it was. A fantastic piece of theater. My staff and I stood at a distance. I held the [detonator]. . . . After prolonging the suspense for a moment, I shouted, "Heil Hitler"; and pressed the button. . . . [T]he fiery explosion soared toward the clouds, an unforgettable tribute to our triumph over the Jews.[11]*

On May 16, 1943, Stroop's daily report summed up the Warsaw ghetto operation in one famous phrase: "The Jewish quarter of Warsaw is no more!"[12]

The Executioner's Fate

After the war, Stroop created a false identity to evade arrest. Though it protected him for a time, he was eventually identified. Both the United States and Poland put him on trial. Both found him guilty and sentenced him to death, but it fell to the Poles to carry out the sentence. On March 6, 1952, Jurgen Joseph Stroop ascended a gallows in Warsaw, where he was hanged for crimes against humanity. To the best of anyone's knowledge, he still believed that, as a member of the "master race," he had done no wrong.

****

At first glance, it may seem impossible that Nazi killers like Jurgen Stroop should have anything in common with

A woman lights a candle at the Warsaw Ghetto Memorial on April 18, 2004, marking the 61st anniversary of the uprising. Although the Jewish fighters were defeated during the battle, the Warsaw ghetto uprising became a lasting symbol of resistance during the Holocaust.

ZOB freedom fighters, or with unwilling officials like Adam Czerniakow, who tried to save Jewish lives by working with the occupational government. Certainly these people were very different from one another, but all of them, Stroop included, did share one thing in common: They were all caught up in events that made heroes of a group of partisans, who fought a hopeless battle against a vastly superior force.

THE WARSAW GHETTO IN CONTEXT

Though German troops crushed the ZOB, they could not destroy its legacy. The uprising demonstrated Jewish courage in the face of overwhelming odds. In the process, it showed that a small force, using hit-and-run tactics, could inflict considerable damage on a powerful enemy.

In Bialystok, Vilna, Krakow, and many other ghettos in Nazi-occupied Europe, Jews got the message. They fought rather than march quietly to the deportation trains. Like the Jews of Warsaw, they did not win. Most of them died in the effort. Still, the uprisings struck a blow against the German forces that were already floundering.

The German defeat at Stalingrad (Russia) had smashed Nazi hopes of conquering the Soviet Union. With American and British forces closing from the west, the war was a lost cause. Even then, Hitler refused to stop killing Jews. In fact, the pace of destruction increased. Soldiers who could have been fighting the war spent their time rounding up Jews. Trains that could have carried troops and supplies to the front lines carried Jewish men, women, and children to the death camps.

The uprisings in Warsaw and other ghettos were not large enough to cost Germany the war, but they did force the Nazis to divert resources to the "final solution." In a small way, that contributed to the defeat of Germany and the failure of Nazi plans to kill all the Jews of Europe.

1939

September 1—Germany invades Poland; World War II begins.

September 23—Adam Czerniakow is appointed chairman of the Jewish Council.

September 27—Warsaw formally surrenders to the Germans.

November 4—The Germans take hostages to ensure "good behavior" in the ghetto.

1940

October 12—Warsaw ghetto is established.

November 16—Ghetto is sealed behind eleven-foot walls.

1942

July 22—Great deportation from Warsaw ghetto begins.

July 23—Adam Czerniakow commits suicide rather than deport thousands of Jews.

July 28—Youth group leaders form the ZOB.

September 10—The great deportation ends.

November—Mordechai Anielewicz becomes commander of the ZOB.

1943

January 18—January uprising begins; lasts four days.

April 19—Germans attack the ghetto in force and the uprising begins.

April 25—Germans begin burning the ghetto.

May 8—Germans destroy ZOB headquarters at Mila 18; the command staff commits suicide.

May 10—Small groups of fighters escape through the sewers.

May 16—Stroop announces the end of the uprising.

Chapter 1. **Adam Czerniakow: The Chairman**

1. Adam Czerniakow, edited by Raul Hilberg, *The Warsaw Diary of Adam Czerniakow: Prelude to Doom* (New York: Stein and Day, Scarborough ed., 1982), p. 87.
2. Ibid., p. 95.
3. Ibid., pp. 212–213.
4. Michal Grynberg, ed., *Words to Outlive Us: Eyewitness Accounts from the Warsaw Ghetto* (New York: Henry Holt and Company, 2002), p. 10.
5. Czerniakow, p. 384.
6. Quoted in "Dignity and Defiance: The Confrontation of Life and Death in the Warsaw Ghetto," The Simon Wiesenthal Center, 1998, <http://motlc.wiesenthal.com/site/pp.aspx?c=ivKVLcMVIsG&b=476119> (May 17, 2010).
7. Chaim A. Kaplan, *Scroll of Agony: The Warsaw Diary of Chaim A. Kaplan* (New York: Collier Books, 1973), pp. 196, 384.

Chapter 2. **Mordechai Anielewicz: The Commander**

1. "Warsaw Ghetto Uprising," United States Holocaust Memorial Museum (USHMM), April 1, 2010, <http://www.ushmm.org/wlc/article.php?ModuleId=10005188> (May 17, 2010).
2. Quoted in Israel Gutman, *Resistance: The Warsaw Ghetto Uprising* (New York: Houghton Mifflin Company, 1994), p. 170.
3. "Call to resistance by the Jewish Fighting Organization in the Warsaw Ghetto, January 1943," Yad Vashem: Documents of the Holocaust, 2004, <http://www1.yadvashem.org/remembrance/rememberance_day/documents/doc138.html> (January 31, 2010).
4. "The Last Letter From Mordecai Anielewicz, Warsaw Ghetto Revolt Commander," Yad Vashem: Documents of the Holocaust, 2004, <http://www1.yadvashem.org/remembrance/rememberance_day/documents/doc145.html> (January 29, 2010).

Chapter 3. Yitzhak Zuckerman: An Ongoing Struggle

1. Yitzhak Zuckerman, *A Surplus of Memory: Chronicle of the Warsaw Ghetto Uprising* (Berkeley, Calif.: University of California Press, 1993), p. 18.
2. Ibid., p. 40.
3. Theodor Herzl, "Excerpts from Herzl's *The Jewish State*," Jewish Virtual Library, 2010, <http://www.jewishvirtuallibrary.org/jsource/Zionism/herzlex.html> (May 17, 2010).
4. Zuckerman, p. 150.
5. Yitzhak Zuckerman, "Testimony in the trial of Adolf Eichmann," The Nizkor Project, Jerusalem, Israel 1961, 1991–2009, <http://www.nizkor.org/ftp.cgi/people/e/eichmann.adolf/transcripts/ftp.py?people/e/eichmann.adolf/transcripts/Sessions/Session-025-06> (May 17, 2010).
6. Zuckerman, p. 283.
7. Quoted in Israel Gutman, *Resistance: The Warsaw Ghetto Uprising* (New York: Houghton Mifflin Company, 1994), p. 183.
8. Zuckerman, p. 377.
9. Ibid., pp. 557–558.

Chapter 4. Zivia Lubetkin: Comrade in Arms

1. "The Promise, The Revolt, The Vow," Lubetkin & Co. Communications, reproduced by permission from the Ghetto Fighters' House, 2006, <www.lubetkin.net/promise.htm> (June 28, 2009).
2. Ibid.
3. Ibid.
4. Quoted in Y. E. Bell, "The Warsaw Ghetto Uprising: Although They Were Ultimately Overwhelmed, the Jews Involved in the Warsaw Ghetto Uprising Fought Valiantly to Regain Their Freedom and Escape Nazi Oppression," *The New American*, vol. 18, January 14, 2002, p. 32.
5. "The Promise, The Revolt, The Vow."
6. Quoted in "1943: Death and Resistance," *The Holocaust Chronicle PROLOGUE: Roots of the Holocaust*, 2009, <http://www.holocaustchronicle.org/staticpages/405.html> (July 2, 2009).
7. Ibid.

8. Quoted in Sheila Segal, *Women of Valor: Stories of Great Jewish Women Who Helped to Shape the Twentieth Century* (West Orange, N.J.: Behrman House, 1996), p. 46.

9. Quoted in Israel Gutman, *Resistance: The Warsaw Ghetto Uprising* (New York: Houghton Mifflin Company, 1994), p. 185.

10. Segal, p. 48.

11. "The Promise, The Revolt, The Vow."

12. Quoted in Dan Kurzman, *The Bravest Battle: The 28 Days of the Warsaw Ghetto Uprising* (Los Angeles: Pinnacle Books edition, 1978), p. 370.

Chapter 5. Simha Rotem: A Man Called Kazik

1. Kazik (Simha Rotem), *Memoirs of a Warsaw Ghetto Fighter* (New Haven, Conn.: Yale University Press, 1994), p. 4.

2. Ibid., pp. 10–11.

3. Sheryl Ochayon, "The Female Couriers During the Holocaust," Yad Vashem, 2010, <http://www1.yadvashem.org/yv/en/education/newsletter/18/couriers.asp#11> (April 30, 2010).

4. Rotem, p. 11.

5. Ibid., p. 14.

6. Ibid., pp. 17–18.

7. Ibid., pp. 28–29.

8. Ibid., p. 33.

9. Ibid., p. 34.

10. Ibid., p. 38.

11. Ibid., pp. 50–51.

12. Quoted from Vered Levy-Barzalia, "The rebels among us," *Haaretz.com*, February 18, 2007, <www.haaretz.com/hasen/spages/773369.html> (May 17, 2010).

Chapter 6. Vladka Meed: Underground Courier

1. Vladka Meed, "Jewish Resistance in the Warsaw Ghetto," *Dimensions*, vol. 7, no. 2, 1993, <http://mandelproject.us/VladkaMeedArticle.doc> (October 15, 2009).

2. Ibid.

3. Quoted in Vladka Meed, *On Both Sides of the Wall* (Washington, D.C.: Holocaust Library, United States Holocaust Memorial Museum, 1993), p. 13.

4. Ibid., pp. 38–39.

5. Quoted from the transcript of an oral interview, "Personal Stories: Individuals—Vladka Meed," United States Holocaust Memorial Museum (USHMM), n.d., <http://www.ushmm.org/museum/exhibit/online/phistories/> (May 20, 2010).
6. Meed, *On Both Sides of the Wall*, p. 69.
7. Ibid., pp. 73–74.
8. Meed, "Jewish Resistance in the Warsaw Ghetto."
9. Ibid.
10. Meed, *On Both Sides of the Wall*, p. 143.
11. Ibid., p. 147.

Chapter 7. Marek Edelman: The Last Commander

1. Marek Edelman, *The Ghetto Fights* (London: Bookmarks, 1990), p. 36.
2. Ibid., p. 39.
3. Ibid., pp. 50–51.
4. Ibid., pp. 51–52.
5. Quoted in Hanna Krall, *Shielding the Flame: An Intimate Conversation with Dr. Marek Edelman, the Last Surviving Leader of the Warsaw Ghetto Uprising* (New York: Henry Holt and Company, 1986), pp. 7–8.
6. Quoted in Lennart Lindskog, "Choosing a way to die—A conversation with Marek Edelman, the only surviving leader of the Warsaw ghetto uprising," 1995–2007, <www.torah.org/features/first person/livingtestimony.html> (November 29, 2009).
7. Quoted in Adam Mickiewicz Institute, "People, Biographical Profiles: Marek Edelman," Diapositive Information Service, 2008–2009, <http://www.diapozytyw.pl/en/site/ludzie/marek_edelman> (December 1, 2009).
8. Krall, p. 6.
9. Ibid., p. 10.
10. Lindskog.
11. Adam Mickiewicz Institute.

Chapter 8. General Jurgen Stroop: The Executioner

1. Kazimierz Moczarski, *Conversations With an Executioner* (Englewood Cliffs, N.J.: Prentice-Hall, Inc., 1981), p. 13.

2. Ibid., p. 21.
3. Ibid.
4. Ibid., p. 92.
5. Ibid., p. 119.
6. Jurgen Stroop, *The Stroop Report*, English Translation (New York: Random House, Inc., 1979), p. 10.
7. Stroop, "Daily Reports," entry for May 8, 1943.
8. Ibid.
9. Ibid.
10. Moczarski, p. 164.
11. Ibid.
12. Stroop, "Daily Reports," entry for May 16, 1943.

aktion—German for "action"; used for operations in which Jews were harassed or rounded up and sent to work camps or death camps.

annihilation—Total or complete destruction.

"Aryan"—A term misused by the Nazis to refer to a person of pure-blooded Germanic background, typically tall, blond, and blue eyed.

blitzkrieg—German for "lightning war," an all-out offensive, designed to overwhelm an enemy in a short period of time.

bunker—A hidden, underground shelter.

concentration camp—A prison for civilians, political prisoners, and all "enemies" of the Nazis, including Jews.

Eretz Israel—Hebrew, literally "land of Israel," the Zionist term for Palestine.

Gentile—A non-Jewish person.

Gestapo—Literally, the *Geheime Staatspolizei*, the Nazi "state secret police," an internal police unit responsible for identifying traitors and people of "questionable loyalty."

guerilla—A fighting unit, or member of such a unit that harasses a more powerful enemy and carries out acts of sabotage.

jackboots—Heavy, calf-high military boots, worn by German soldiers.

Judenrat—German word for Jewish council appointed by the Nazis to keep the Jewish community under control.

liquidate—The term the Nazis used to mean "complete destruction." Sometimes the term was used to describe an action in which only some residents were either killed or transported to a death camp. In this case, the action was usually a step toward total destruction of the ghetto.

occupational government—A government run by a conquering enemy power.

partisan—A band of fighters that harasses an enemy with small-scale, surprise attacks. During World War II, these groups often hid in the forests.

pogrom—A brutal and violent action usually aimed at a particular ethnic or religious group.

"resettlement"—In the ghettos, a Nazi term for sending trainloads of Jews to supposed work camps.

Russian front—The site of Germany's war against the Soviet Union, beginning June 22, 1941.

***Schutzstaffel* (SS)**—A security unit responsible for administration of the ghettos.

training kibbutz—Collective farm where European Jews trained for life in Eretz Israel.

underground—A political or paramilitary organization that operates in secret.

Yiddish—Folk language of Eastern European Jews; a blend of Hebrew with German and other European languages.

Zionism—A movement that sought to establish a Jewish homeland in Palestine.

Books

Boraks-Nemetz, Lilian and Irene N. Watts, eds. *Tapestry of Hope: Holocaust Writing for Young People*. Plattsburg, N.Y.: Tundra Books of Northern New York, 2003.

Downing, David. *Fighting Back*. Milwaukee, Wis.: World Almanac Library, 2006.

Kacer, Kathy and Sharon E. McKay. *Whispers From the Ghettos*. London: Puffin Books, 2009.

Kazik (Simha Rotem). *Memoirs of a Warsaw Ghetto Fighter*. New Haven, Conn.: Yale University Press, 2002.

Nir, Yehuda. *The Lost Childhood: The Complete Memoir*. Tucson, Ariz.: Schaffner Press, Inc., 2007.

Zapruder, Alexandra, ed. *Salvaged Pages: Young Writers' Diaries of the Holocaust*. New Haven, Conn.: Yale University Press, 2002.

Internet Adresses

Ghetto Fighters' House Museum
   <http://www.gfh.org.il/eng/>

United States Holocaust Memorial Museum
   <http://www.ushmm.org/>

Yad Vashem, The Holocaust Martyrs'
   and Heroes' Remembrance Authority
   <http://www.yadvashem.org/>